William Shakespeare's
Macbeth
In Plain and Simple English

C000055720

BookCaps Study Guides
www.SwipeSpeare.com

About This Series

About This Series

The "Classic Retold" series started as a way of telling classics for the modern reader—being careful to preserve the themes and integrity of the original. Whether you want to understand Shakespeare a little more or are trying to get a better grasps of the Greek classics, there is a book waiting for you!

The series is expanding every month. Visit BookCaps.com to see all the books in the series, and while you are there join the Facebook page, so you are first to know when a new book comes out.

Characters

DUNCAN, King of Scotland

MALCOLM, his Son

DONALBAIN, his Son

MACBETH, General in the King's Army

BANQUO, General in the King's Army

MACDUFF, Nobleman of Scotland

LENNOX, Nobleman of Scotland

ROSS, Nobleman of Scotland

MENTEITH, Nobleman of Scotland

ANGUS, Nobleman of Scotland

CAITHNESS, Nobleman of Scotland

FLEANCE, Son to Banquo

SIWARD, Earl of Northumberland, General of the English Forces

YOUNG SIWARD, his Son

SEYTON, an Officer attending on Macbeth

BOY, Son to Macduff

An English Docto

A Scotch Doctor

A Soldier

A Porter

An Old Man

Comparative Version

Act I

Scene I

A Desert Place

Thunder and lightning. Enter three Witches

First Witch
When shall we three meet again
In thunder, lightning, or in rain?

When will the three of us meet again?
Will there be thunder, lightning or rain?

Second Witch
When the hurlyburly's done,
When the battle's lost and won.

We will meet when the commotion is over.
We will meet when the battle has been lost or won.

Third Witch
That will be ere the set of sun.

That will be before the sun sets.

First Witch
Where the place?

Where will we meet?

Second Witch
Upon the heath.

We'll meet in the open field.

Third Witch
There to meet with Macbeth.

We'll meet Macbeth there.

First Witch
I come, Graymalkin!

I'm coming, Graymalkin, gray cat of mine!

Second Witch
Paddock calls.

Paddock, my frog, calls me, too!

Third Witch
Anon.

Soon!

ALL
Fair is foul, and foul is fair:
Hover through the fog and filthy air.

Beautiful is ugly, and ugly is beautiful.
Let us float through the fog and filthy air.

Exeunt

Exit.

Scene II

A Camp Near Forres.

Alarum within. Enter DUNCAN, MALCOLM, DONALBAIN, LENNOX, with Attendants, meeting a bleeding Sergeant

DUNCAN
What bloody man is that? He can report,
As seemeth by his plight, of the revolt
The newest state.

Who is this wounded man?
It seems he can report on the current
state of the battle.

MALCOLM
This is the sergeant
Who like a good and hardy soldier fought
'Gainst my captivity. Hail, brave friend!
 Say to the king the knowledge of the broil
As thou didst leave it.

He is a sergeant, who fought like a strong
and good soldier to keep me from capture.
My brave friend!
Tell the king what you know
of the war when you left it.

Sergeant
Doubtful it stood;
As two spent swimmers, that do cling together
And choke their art. The merciless Macdonwald--
Worthy to be a rebel, for to that
The multiplying villanies of nature
Do swarm upon him--from the western isles
Of kerns and gallowglasses is supplied;
And fortune, on his damned quarrel smiling,
Show'd like a rebel's whore: but all's too weak:
For brave Macbeth--well he deserves that name--
Disdaining fortune, with his brandish'd steel,
Which smoked with bloody execution,
Like valour's minion carved out his passage
Till he faced the slave;
Which ne'er shook hands, nor bade farewell to him,
Till he unseam'd him from the nave to the chaps,
And fix'd his head upon our battlements.

It was doubtful, just like two exhausted
swimmers who cling. to each other and choke
one another. Macdonwald was like a rebel
with many forces of nature in him. He had a
ready supply of foot soldiers and massive
warriors. Fortune smiled on his damned war,
and looked just like a rebel's whore. But
fortune was not strong enough. Brave
Macbeth— he deserves that name—went
against fortune with his sword drawn, and he
cut through it all with blood until he faced
Macdonwald. He didn't even shake hands or
say goodbye to him. He just cut him in two,
and put Macdonwald's head on our fort's
wall.

DUNCAN
O valiant cousin! worthy gentleman!

Oh, my brave cousin! What a worthy man!

Sergeant
As whence the sun 'gins his reflection
Shipwrecking storms and direful thunders break,
So from that spring whence comfort
seem'd to come
Discomfort swells. Mark, king of Scotland, mark:

Just like when the sun rises and storms
capable of wrecking ships and awful thunder
end— that place where comfort
seemed to
come, instead discomfort came. Listen to me,

No sooner justice had with valour arm'd
Compell'd these skipping kerns to trust their heels,
But the Norweyan lord surveying vantage,
With furbish'd arms and new supplies of men
Began a fresh assault.

king of Scotland, listen: No sooner did justice come armed with courage, causing the foot soldiers to start running away, did the Norwegian lord see his chance to bring in more arms and new soldiers and begin a fresh attack.

DUNCAN
Dismay'd not this
Our captains, Macbeth and Banquo?

Didn't this worry our captains, Macbeth and Banquo?

Sergeant
Yes;
As sparrows eagles, or the hare the lion.
If I say sooth, I must report they were
As cannons overcharged with double cracks,
so they
Doubly redoubled strokes upon the foe:
Except they meant to bathe in reeking wounds,
Or memorise another Golgotha,
I cannot tell.
But I am faint, my gashes cry for help.

Yes, it did. Like it would worry sparrows before the eagle, or lambs before the lion. I swear, they were like cannons overcharged with cracks—they doubled twice over their attacks against the enemy: whether they aimed for a bloodbath or a second Crucifixion, who knows? I am faint and my wounds need tending.

DUNCAN
So well thy words become thee as thy wounds;

Your words speak as highly of you as your wounds.

They smack of honour both. Go get him surgeons.

They speak of your honor. Go, and get him doctors.

Exit Sergeant, attended

Who comes here?

Who is coming?

Enter ROSS

MALCOLM
The worthy thane of Ross.

It is the worthy Thane of Ross.

LENNOX
What a haste looks through his eyes!
So should he look
That seems to speak things strange.

*He has such a hurried look about him!
And looking that way,
Has so many strange things to say.*

ROSS
God save the king!

God save the king!

DUNCAN
Whence camest thou, worthy thane?

Where have you come from, worthy thane?

ROSS
From Fife, great king;
Where the Norweyan banners flout the sky
And fan our people cold. Norway himself,
With terrible numbers,
Assisted by that most disloyal traitor
The thane of Cawdor, began a dismal conflict;
Till that Bellona's bridegroom, lapp'd in proof,
Confronted him with self-comparisons,
Point against point rebellious, arm 'gainst arm.
Curbing his lavish spirit: and, to conclude,
The victory fell on us.

DUNCAN
Great happiness!

ROSS
That now
Sweno, the Norways' king, craves composition:
Nor would we deign him burial of his men
Till he disbursed at Saint Colme's inch
Ten thousand dollars to our general use.

DUNCAN
No more that thane of Cawdor shall deceive
Our bosom interest: go pronounce his present death,
And with his former title greet Macbeth.

ROSS
I'll see it done.

DUNCAN
What he hath lost noble Macbeth hath won.

Exeunt

I've come from Fife, great King,
where the Norwegian flags fly
chilling our people. The King of Norway
was there with great numbers of men.
The thane of Cawdor began a conflict
until the war's bridegroom himself,
wrapped in truth, confronted him with
comparisons, pointing out how they were both
rebellious, and both armed well,
and it stopped his extravagant spirit and the
victory fell to us.

It makes me so happy to hear this!

After that, Sweno, Norway's king, wanted an
agreement, but we would not allow his men to
be buried until he paid us ten thousand
dollars at Saint Colme's.

The thane of Cawdor will no longer betray
the things important to us: order his death
immediately.
And give his former title to Macbeth.

I'll see that it's done.

What he has lost, the noble Macbeth has won.

Scene III

A Heath Near Forres

Thunder. Enter the three Witches

First Witch
Where hast thou been, sister?

Where have you been, sister?

Second Witch
Killing swine.

Killing pigs.

Third Witch
Sister, where thou?

Where were you killing them, sister?

First Witch
A sailor's wife had chestnuts in her lap,
And munch'd, and munch'd, and munch'd:--
'Give me,' quoth I:
'Aroint thee, witch!' the rump-fed ronyon cries.
Her husband's to Aleppo gone, master o' the Tiger:

But in a sieve I'll thither sail,
And, like a rat without a tail,
I'll do, I'll do, and I'll do.

A sailor's wife had chestnuts in her lap.
That she ate, and ate, and ate.
'Give me some,' I said.
'Get out of here, witch!' the fat hag said.
Her husband had gone to see Allepo, the
master of the Tiger.
I will sail there in a vessel with holes,
and like a tail-less rat,
I'll do, and I'll do, and I'll do harm.

Second Witch
I'll give thee a wind.

I will provide you with a wind!

First Witch
Thou'rt kind.

You are kind.

Third Witch
And I another.

I will give you a wind, as well.

First Witch
I myself have all the other,
And the very ports they blow,
All the quarters that they know
I' the shipman's card.
I will drain him dry as hay:
Sleep shall neither night nor day
Hang upon his pent-house lid;
He shall live a man forbid:

I have all the other winds,
and I have the ports they blow in.
I have all the places that they know,
and I have the ship's direction.
I will drain the sailor dry as hay:
sleep will not come night or day
to the roof of his home.
He will live like a man without:

Weary se'nnights nine times nine
Shall he dwindle, peak and pine:
Though his bark cannot be lost,
Yet it shall be tempest-tost.
Look what I have.

he will go for weeks without rest,
and he will fade and become weak and weary.
But his ship will not be lost—
it will be tossed on a stormy sea.
Look here at what I have.

Second Witch
Show me, show me.

Show me, show me!

First Witch
Here I have a pilot's thumb,
Wreck'd as homeward he did come.

I have a sailor's thumb who died in a
shipwreck as he was coming home.

Drum within

Third Witch
A drum, a drum!
Macbeth doth come.

A drum, a drum!
Macbeth is coming!

ALL
The weird sisters, hand in hand,
Posters of the sea and land,
Thus do go about, about:
Thrice to thine and thrice to mine
And thrice again, to make up nine.
Peace! the charm's wound up.

The three witches, hand in hand,
who know all of sea and land,
thus do go about and about:
three times to you, and three times to me
and three times once more makes nine.
Peace! That spell has been cast.

Enter MACBETH and BANQUO

MACBETH
So foul and fair a day I have not seen.

I have never seen a day so beautiful and ugly
at the same time.

BANQUO
How far is't call'd to Forres? What are these
So wither'd and so wild in their attire,
That look not like the inhabitants o' the earth,
And yet are on't? Live you? or are you aught
That man may question? You seem to understand
me,
By each at once her chappy finger laying
Upon her skinny lips: you should be women,
And yet your beards forbid me to interpret
That you are so.

How far is it to a place called Forres? What
are these creatures so withered and wild
looking that do not even look like they belong
on this earth? And yet they are on it. Are you
alive? Or are you something that we should
wonder about? You seem
to understand me, since you are putting your
gnarled fingers to your thin lips. You seem to
be women, but your beards make me think that
you are not.

MACBETH
Speak, if you can: what are you?

Speak, if you can. What are you?

First Witch
All hail, Macbeth! hail to thee, thane of Glamis!

All hail, Macbeth! Hail to you, Thane of Glamis!

Second Witch
All hail, Macbeth, hail to thee, thane of Cawdor!

All hail, Macbeth! Hail to you, Thane of Cawdor!

Third Witch
All hail, Macbeth, thou shalt be king hereafter!

All hail, Macbeth, you will be king someday!

BANQUO
Good sir, why do you start; and seem to fear
Things that do sound so fair? I' the name of truth,
Are ye fantastical, or that indeed
Which outwardly ye show? My noble partner
You greet with present grace and great prediction
Of noble having and of royal hope,
That he seems rapt withal: to me you speak not.
If you can look into the seeds of time,
And say which grain will grow and which will not,
Speak then to me, who neither beg nor fear
Your favours nor your hate.

My good man, why do you look so upset and afraid to hear things that sound so good? Tell me the truth, are you illusions, or are you real? You greet my friend here with grace and great predictions of having nobility and someday being king. He looks as if he is in a spell! But you do not speak to me.
If you can tell the future and say what will happen to me, then tell me. I do not beg and I am not afraid of your favors or your hate.

First Witch
Hail!

Hail!

Second Witch
Hail!

Hail!

Third Witch
Hail!

Hail!

First Witch
Lesser than Macbeth, and greater.

You will be less than Macbeth, but greater.

Second Witch
Not so happy, yet much happier.

You will not be so happy, but much happier than Macbeth.

Third Witch
Thou shalt get kings, though thou be none:
So all hail, Macbeth and Banquo!

Your sons will be kings, although you will not. All hail, Macbeth and Banquo!

First Witch
Banquo and Macbeth, all hail!

Banquo and Macbeth, all hail!

MACBETH

Stay, you imperfect speakers, tell me more:
By Sinel's death I know I am thane of Glamis;
But how of Cawdor? the thane of Cawdor lives,
A prosperous gentleman; and to be king
Stands not within the prospect of belief,
No more than to be Cawdor. Say from whence
You owe this strange intelligence? or why
Upon this blasted heath you stop our way
With such prophetic greeting? Speak, I charge you.

Wait, you have not told the whole story—say more. I know that by inheritance I am the Thane of Glamis. But how could I be Thane of Cawdor? The Thane of Cawdor lives. And for me to be a wealthy gentleman, and a king, as well—that makes no more sense than my becoming the Thane of Cawdor. Tell me how you know these things? And why have you stopped us in this field with such a prophetic greeting? I demand you say more!

Witches vanish

BANQUO

The earth hath bubbles, as the water has,
And these are of them. Whither are they vanish'd?

The earth has bubbles, just like water does. These spirits were like those bubbles. Where did they go?

MACBETH

Into the air; and what seem'd corporal melted
As breath into the wind. Would they had stay'd!

They vanished into the air, and what seemed solid Faded into nothing. I wish they had stayed!

BANQUO

Were such things here as we do speak about?
Or have we eaten on the insane root
That takes the reason prisoner?

Did we really see them? Or have we been drugged, and are hallucinating?

MACBETH

Your children shall be kings.

Your children will be kings.

BANQUO

You shall be king.

You will be king.

MACBETH

And thane of Cawdor too: went it not so?

And Thane of Cawdor, too. Didn't they say that?

BANQUO

To the selfsame tune and words. Who's here?

That's what I heard. Who's here?

Enter ROSS and ANGUS

ROSS

The king hath happily received, Macbeth,
The news of thy success; and when he reads
Thy personal venture in the rebels' fight,
His wonders and his praises do contend
Which should be thine or his: silenced with that,

The king was happy to hear of your success, Macbeth, and when he heard of your feats in the fight, he was so amazed and full of praise that he wondered what should be yours and what should be his. The tale rendered him

In viewing o'er the rest o' the selfsame day,
He finds thee in the stout Norweyan ranks,
Nothing afeard of what thyself didst make,
Strange images of death. As thick as hail
Came post with post; and every one did bear
Thy praises in his kingdom's great defence,
And pour'd them down before him.

ANGUS
We are sent
To give thee from our royal master thanks;
Only to herald thee into his sight,
Not pay thee.

ROSS
And, for an earnest of a greater honour,
He bade me, from him, call thee thane of Cawdor:
In which addition, hail, most worthy thane!
For it is thine.

BANQUO
What, can the devil speak true?

MACBETH
The thane of Cawdor lives: why do you dress me
In borrow'd robes?

ANGUS
Who was the thane lives yet;
But under heavy judgment bears that life
Which he deserves to lose. Whether he was combined
With those of Norway, or did line the rebel
With hidden help and vantage, or that with both
He labour'd in his country's wreck, I know not;
But treasons capital, confess'd and proved,
Have overthrown him.

MACBETH
[Aside] Glamis, and thane of Cawdor!

The greatest is behind.

To ROSS and ANGUS

Thanks for your pains.

speechless, and then he heard about the rest of the day—how you found yourself fighting the strong Norwegian soldiers with no fear of death although images of it were all around you. Like a noisy hail storm, the messengers arrived one after another singing your praises to the king.

*We have been sent
to give you the king's thanks
We are not to pay you, but must bring you to him.*

And for a hint at the great honor you will receive, he told me, from him, to call you Thane of Cawdor: and also to hail you, worthy thane! The title is yours.

What? Does the devil speak the truth?

The Thane of Cawdor lives—why do you give Me the title that is his?

*He was the thane and is still alive,
but he has been judged not worthy to live.*

Whether he joined with those of Norway, or provided the rebels with secret help and advantage, or did both, it doesn't matter. He played a part in his country's destruction. His treason has been confessed and proved and it has overthrown him.

*[Aside] First Glamis, and now the Thane of Cawdor!
The most unlikely has passed.*

Thank you for your trouble.

To BANQUO
Do you not hope your children shall be kings,
When those that gave the thane of Cawdor to me
Promised no less to them?

BANQUO
That trusted home
Might yet enkindle you unto the crown,
Besides the thane of Cawdor. But 'tis strange:

And oftentimes, to win us to our harm,

The instruments of darkness tell us truths,
Win us with honest trifles, to betray's
In deepest consequence.
Cousins, a word, I pray you.

MACBETH
[Aside] Two truths are told,
As happy prologues to the swelling act
Of the imperial theme.--I thank you, gentlemen.

Aside
This supernatural soliciting
Cannot be ill, cannot be good: if ill,
Why hath it given me earnest of success,
Commencing in a truth? I am thane of Cawdor:

If good, why do I yield to that suggestion
Whose horrid image doth unfix my hair
And make my seated heart knock at my ribs,

Against the use of nature? Present fears
Are less than horrible imaginings:
My thought, whose murder yet is but fantastical,

Shakes so my single state of man that function
Is smother'd in surmise, and nothing is
But what is not.

BANQUO
Look, how our partner's rapt.

MACBETH
[Aside] If chance will have me king,

Do you not now have hope that your children will be kings, when those that gave the title of Thane of Cawdor promised no less to them?

*That prophecy, if trusted, might inspire passion in you to become king as well as the Thane of Cawdor. But, it's strange:
often, in order to win our trust so they can harm us,
the instruments of darkness will tell us a little of the truth, only to betray us and cause deep consequence.
Cousins, may I speak with you?*

[Aside] Two truths have been told, and are happy indications that I may become king. Thank you, gentlemen.

*This supernatural news can't be bad, and it can't be good. If bad, then why has it given me the promise of success beginning in the truth? I am Thane of Cawdor.
If good, why do I yield to a suggestion whose horrid image unfixes my hair and causes my heart to pound harder in my chest
than what is natural? My present fears are less that horrible imaginings:
My thought, whose murder is still just a fantasy,
Shakes me so that functioning as a man is smothered in things that are supposed. Nothing is, only what is not.*

Look at how our friend is distracted.

[Aside] If chance is to have me be king,

why, chance may crown me,
Without my stir.

then chance will crown me
without my doing a thing.

BANQUO
New honors come upon him,
Like our strange garments,
cleave not to their mould
But with the aid of use.

New honors have come upon him,
like new clothes
that only fit after they have been worn awhile.

MACBETH
[Aside] Come what come may,
Time and the hour runs through the roughest day.

[Aside] What ever will happen will happen,
time keeps on even through the roughest day.

BANQUO
Worthy Macbeth, we stay upon your leisure.

Good Macbeth, we wait for you.

MACBETH
Give me your favour: my dull brain was wrought
With things forgotten. Kind gentlemen, your pains
Are register'd where every day I turn
The leaf to read them. Let us toward the king.
Think upon what hath chanced, and, at more time,
The interim having weigh'd it, let us speak
Our free hearts each to other.

Please beg my pardon; I was deep in thought
with things forgotten. Kind gentlemen, the
trouble you took today is recorded in my
mind, and when I think back to this day, I will
remember this. Let us go see the king. Keep in
mind what has happened, and when time has
passed and we have considered it, let us speak
what is in our hearts to one another.

BANQUO
Very gladly.

That sounds good.

MACBETH
Till then, enough. Come, friends.

Until then, enough. Come, friends, let's go.

Exeunt

18

Scene IV

Forres. The Palace.

Flourish. Enter DUNCAN, MALCOLM, DONALBAIN, LENNOX, and Attendants

DUNCAN
Is execution done on Cawdor? Are not
Those in commission yet return'd?

Has Cawdor been killed yet? Have those sent to do the job returned?

MALCOLM
My liege,
They are not yet come back. But I have spoke
With one that saw him die: who did report
That very frankly he confess'd his treasons,
Implored your highness' pardon and set forth
A deep repentance: nothing in his life
Became him like the leaving it; he died
As one that had been studied in his death
To throw away the dearest thing he owed,
As 'twere a careless trifle.

My lord, they have not come back yet. But I spoke with someone who saw him die, and they said that he frankly confessed his treasons, begged your forgiveness and said he was deeply sorry: nothing in his life became him like the leaving of it; he died like someone who had learned how to throw away the dearest thing he owned as if it were nothing.

DUNCAN
There's no art
To find the mind's construction in the face:
He was a gentleman on whom I built
An absolute trust.

There's no way to find the truth of someone in their face. He was a man whom I trusted completely.

Enter MACBETH, BANQUO, ROSS, and ANGUS

O worthiest cousin!
The sin of my ingratitude even now
Was heavy on me: thou art so far before
That swiftest wing of recompense is slow
To overtake thee. Would thou hadst less deserved,
That the proportion both of thanks and payment
Might have been mine! only I have left to say,
More is thy due than more than all can pay.

My best cousin! The guilt of being able to thank you enough was just weighing heavy on me: you are so deserving of reward it can not come to you fast enough. If you had deserved less, then the gratitude and payment might have been easier! All I can say it that you deserve more than we can ever give to you.

MACBETH
The service and the loyalty I owe,
In doing it, pays itself. Your highness' part
Is to receive our duties; and our duties
Are to your throne and state children and servants,

The service and loyalty I owe repays itself. Your highness's part is to receive our duties, and our duties are to your throne and children and servants. We do what we

Which do but what they should, by doing every thing
Safe toward your love and honour.

DUNCAN
Welcome hither:
I have begun to plant thee, and will labour
To make thee full of growing. Noble Banquo,
That hast no less deserved, nor must be known
No less to have done so, let me enfold thee
And hold thee to my heart.

BANQUO
There if I grow,
The harvest is your own.

DUNCAN
My plenteous joys,
Wanton in fulness, seek to hide themselves
In drops of sorrow. Sons, kinsmen, thanes,
And you whose places are the nearest, know
We will establish our estate upon
Our eldest, Malcolm, whom we name hereafter
The Prince of Cumberland; which honour must
Not unaccompanied invest him only,
But signs of nobleness, like stars, shall shine
On all deservers. From hence to Inverness,
And bind us further to you.

MACBETH
The rest is labour, which is not used for you:
I'll be myself the harbinger and make joyful
The hearing of my wife with your approach;
So humbly take my leave.

DUNCAN
My worthy Cawdor!

MACBETH
[Aside] The Prince of Cumberland! that is a step

On which I must fall down, or else o'erleap,
For in my way it lies. Stars, hide your fires;
Let not light see my black and deep desires:
The eye wink at the hand; yet let that be,

should by doing all things toward your

love and honor.

Welcome here.
I have nurtured your career and will strive
to make it fully grown. Noble Banquo,
you are no less deserving and should not
receive no less honor for doing what you did.
Let me bring you into my fold and hold you in
my heart.

If I grow there
it is to your credit.

My joy is so great it brings tears to my eyes.
Sons, kinsmen, thanes, and others who are
near, witness today that I will establish my
kingdom upon my oldest son, Malcolm, who
will now be known as the Prince of
Cumberland. But he is not the only one
to be honored. Nobility, like stars, shines on
all deserving. Let us go to Inverness, where I
will be your guest,

I am so eager to be working for you that
resting is hard work. I will tell my wife
the joyful news of your arrival.
Allow me to take my leave.

My worthy Cawdor!

[Aside] The Prince of Cumberland! That is a step
on which I must fall, or else overcome,
for it lies in my way. Stars, hide your light;
do not shine on my deep and dark desires.
The eye may blink at the hand, yet when it is over

Which the eye fears, when it is done, to see.

Exit

DUNCAN
True, worthy Banquo; he is full so valiant,
And in his commendations I am fed;
It is a banquet to me. Let's after him,
Whose care is gone before to bid us welcome:
It is a peerless kinsman.

Flourish. Exeunt

the eye will see what it fears.

It's true, my good Banquo, he is so valiant and there is much to commend him. It satisfies me. Let's follow him. He has taken care to go ahead and prepare for us. There are very few as good as him.

Scene V

Inverness. Macbeth's Castle.

Enter LADY MACBETH, reading a letter

LADY MACBETH
'They met me in the day of success: and I have
learned by the perfectest report, they have more in
them than mortal knowledge. When I burned in
desire
to question them further, they made themselves air,
into which they vanished. Whiles I stood rapt in
the wonder of it, came missives from the king, who
all-hailed me 'Thane of Cawdor;' by which title,
before, these weird sisters saluted me, and referred
me to the coming on of time, with 'Hail, king that
shalt be!' This have I thought good to deliver
thee, my dearest partner of greatness, that thou
mightst not lose the dues of rejoicing, by being
ignorant of what greatness is promised thee. Lay it
to thy heart, and farewell.'
Glamis thou art, and Cawdor; and shalt be
What thou art promised: yet do I fear thy nature;
It is too full o' the milk of human kindness
To catch the nearest way: thou wouldst be great;
Art not without ambition, but without
The illness should attend it: what thou wouldst
highly,
That wouldst thou holily; wouldst not play false,
And yet wouldst wrongly win: thou'ldst have,
great Glamis,
That which cries 'Thus thou must do,
if thou have it;
And that which rather thou dost fear to do
Than wishest should be undone.' Hie thee hither,
That I may pour my spirits in thine ear;
And chastise with the valour of my tongue
All that impedes thee from the golden round,
Which fate and metaphysical aid doth seem
To have thee crown'd withal.

*'They met me on the day of success: and I
have learned in the most perfect way that they
know more than men. When I tried to question
them further, they vanished into the air. While
I stood in wonder, messengers sent by the king
arrived and hailed me as the 'Thane of
Cawdor;' which is exactly what the witches
called me, saying as well that I will be king
someday. I wanted to let you know all of this,
my dearest partner of greatness, so that you
may not lose out on the rejoicing by not
knowing of the greatness that is promised us.
Hold it in your heart and tell no one,
farewell.'*

*You are the thane of Glamis and Cawdor, and
you will be king, as promised. But I fear your
nature is too kind to grab the opportunity. It's
not that you are without ambition, it's just that
you do not possess the malevolence required
for it: you would rather take the high road
and do good
things; you would not lie and you would not
cheat:
to you, great Glamis. You want them, but
you are not willing to do what is necessary
to have them. You wish them done for you.
Hurry home, so that I may say the words
you need to hear to give you strength and
encourage you to banish all that is keeping
you from getting what you want in this golden
round. Fate and supernatural forces both
seem to agree that you should be crowned
king.*

Enter a Messenger

What is your tidings?

What are you here to tell me?

Messenger
The king comes here to-night.

The king is coming here tonight.

LADY MACBETH
Thou'rt mad to say it:
Is not thy master with him? who, were't so,
Would have inform'd for preparation.

You must be crazy.
Is not your master with him? And, if that were
so, he would have informed us to prepare.

Messenger
So please you, it is true: our thane is coming:
One of my fellows had the speed of him,
Who, almost dead for breath, had scarcely more
Than would make up his message.

So help me, it is true: Macbeth is coming.
Another messenger ran all the way here,
and—almost dead, he was so out of breath—
he managed to deliver the message.

LADY MACBETH
Give him tending;
He brings great news.

Tend to him.
He brings great news.

Exit Messenger

The raven himself is hoarse
That croaks the fatal entrance of Duncan
Under my battlements. Come, you spirits
That tend on mortal thoughts, unsex me here,
And fill me from the crown to the toe top-full
Of direst cruelty! make thick my blood;
Stop up the access and passage to remorse,
That no compunctious visitings of nature
Shake my fell purpose, nor keep peace between
The effect and it! Come to my woman's breasts,
And take my milk for gall, you murdering ministers,
Wherever in your sightless substances
You wait on nature's mischief! Come, thick night,
And pall thee in the dunnest smoke of hell,
That my keen knife see not the wound it makes,
Nor heaven peep through the blanket of the dark,
To cry 'Hold, hold!'

The raven himself is hoarse
who tells of the fatal entrance of Duncan
into my castle. Come, sprits that tend
on mortal thoughts, make me more like a man,
and fill me from head to toe with the worst
cruelty! Make my blood thick,
stop up any feelings of remorse I may have,
so that no regret or guilt may visit me
and shake my sole purpose, or try to stop it.
Come to my motherly breast and make my
milk into poison, you murdering guardians,
wherever you wait unseen to witness
the evil! Come, thick night, and cloak
everything in the darkest smoke of hell,
so that this night does not see the wound it
makes, and heaven can not look through the
darkness and say 'Stop!'

Enter MACBETH

Great Glamis! worthy Cawdor!
Greater than both, by the all-hail hereafter!
Thy letters have transported me beyond
This ignorant present, and I feel now

Great Glamis! Worthy Cawdor!
You are greater than both and will hailed
in the future as king! You letters have taken
me beyond the ignorant present into

The future in the instant.

MACBETH
My dearest love,
Duncan comes here to-night.

LADY MACBETH
And when goes hence?

MACBETH
To-morrow, as he purposes.

LADY MACBETH
O, never
Shall sun that morrow see!
Your face, my thane, is as a book where men
May read strange matters. To beguile the time,
Look like the time; bear welcome in your eye,
Your hand, your tongue:
look like the innocent flower,
But be the serpent under't. He that's coming
Must be provided for: and you shall put
This night's great business into my dispatch;
Which shall to all our nights and days to come
Give solely sovereign sway and masterdom.

MACBETH
We will speak further.

LADY MACBETH
Only look up clear;
To alter favour ever is to fear:
Leave all the rest to me.

Exeunt

the future that feels like it is already here.

My dearest love,
Duncan comes here tonight.

And when does he leave?

He says he will leave tomorrow.

Oh,
never shall the sun see tomorrow!
Your face, my thane, is like a book where one
can read that something is wrong. You need to
look like everything is all right at this time;
bear welcome in your eye, your handshake,
the words you say: look like an innocent
flower, but be the serpent that lies under it. He
is coming and he must be given care. You
should put the night's events in my hands. All
of the nights and days of our future will be
changed by what happens tonight.

We will speak more about this.

You should only appear clear—
to change at all favors fear.
Leave the rest to me.

Scene VI.

Before Macbeth's Castle.

Hautboys and torches. Enter DUNCAN, MALCOLM, DONALBAIN, BANQUO, LENNOX, MACDUFF, ROSS, ANGUS, and Attendants

DUNCAN
This castle hath a pleasant seat; the air
Nimbly and sweetly recommends itself
Unto our gentle senses.

This castle has a good feeling about it. The air is nimble and sweet, and pleases the gentlest senses.

BANQUO
This guest of summer,
The temple-haunting martlet, does approve,
By his loved mansionry, that the heaven's breath
Smells wooingly here: no jutty, frieze,
Buttress, nor coign of vantage, but this bird
Hath made his pendent bed and procreant cradle:
Where they most breed and haunt, I have observed,
The air is delicate.

The summer season bird, the house martin, likes it here. By staying here it proves that the air here is as tempting as heaven's breath. There is no place in the castle the bird has not nested and bred. The house martin tends to favor, by my observation, places where the air is delicate and nice.

Enter LADY MACBETH

DUNCAN
See, see, our honour'd hostess!
The love that follows us sometime is our trouble,
Which still we thank as love. Herein I teach you
How you shall bid God 'ild us for your pains,
And thank us for your trouble.

Look, here comes our honored hostess! Sometimes the love that follows us is trouble, but we still are grateful of the love. Here, I will teach you how to ask God to yield to your pains, and thank us for your trouble.

LADY MACBETH
All our service
In every point twice done and then done double
Were poor and single business to contend
Against those honours deep and broad wherewith
Your majesty loads our house: for those of old,
And the late dignities heap'd up to them,
We rest your hermits.

All of our service, in every way, if it were to be done and done again could not match the deep honor you have brought to us by being here. For the past and new dignities you've heaped on us, we intend can take a break from their praying.

DUNCAN
Where's the thane of Cawdor?
We coursed him at the heels, and had a purpose
To be his purveyor: but he rides well;
And his great love, sharp as his spur, hath holp him
To his home before us. Fair and noble hostess,

Where is Macbeth? We rode right at his heels, but he had purpose to get here first, and he rides well. His great love, sharp as his spur, helped him to get to his castle before us.

We are your guest to-night.

LADY MACBETH
Your servants ever

Have theirs, themselves and what is theirs,
in compt,
To make their audit at your highness' pleasure,
Still to return your own.

DUNCAN
Give me your hand;
Conduct me to mine host: we love him highly,
And shall continue our graces towards him.
By your leave, hostess.

Exeunt

Fair and noble hostess, we are your guests
tonight.

Your servants may help themselves to
whatever
they need to make you comfortable. We are
glad
to be able to give back to you what is yours.

Give me your hand.
Take me to my host. We love him dearly,
and shall continue to offer him good things.
After you, Lady Macbeth.

Scene VII

Macbeth's Castle.

Hautboys and torches. Enter a Sewer, and divers Servants with dishes and service, and pass over the stage. Then enter MACBETH

MACBETH

If it were done when 'tis done, then 'twere well
It were done quickly: if the assassination
Could trammel up the consequence, and catch
With his surcease success; that but this blow
Might be the be-all and the end-all here,
But here, upon this bank and shoal of time,
We'd jump the life to come. But in these cases
We still have judgment here; that we but teach
Bloody instructions, which, being taught, return
To plague the inventor: this even-handed justice
Commends the ingredients of our poison'd chalice
To our own lips. He's here in double trust;
First, as I am his kinsman and his subject,
Strong both against the deed; then, as his host,
Who should against his murderer shut the door,
Not bear the knife myself. Besides, this Duncan
Hath borne his faculties so meek, hath been
So clear in his great office, that his virtues
Will plead like angels, trumpet-tongued, against
The deep damnation of his taking-off;
And pity, like a naked new-born babe,
Striding the blast, or heaven's cherubim, horsed
Upon the sightless couriers of the air,
Shall blow the horrid deed in every eye,
That tears shall drown the wind. I have no spur
To prick the sides of my intent, but only
Vaulting ambition, which o'erleaps itself
And falls on the other.

Enter LADY MACBETH

How now! what news?

LADY MACBETH
He has almost supp'd:
why have you left the chamber?

If it were over when it is over, then it would be best if it were done quickly. If the murder could be without consequence, bringing up only a success, then the blow would be the be-all and the end-all now. And here, upon this bank and this place in time, I'd jump at the chance. But in these sort of situations there will be judgment, and the bloody instructions taught by the murderer will come back to haunt the murderer: this even-handed justice makes for our own death, and we might as well put a poisoned chalice to our own lips. Duncan is here in double trust. First, I am his relative as well as his subject, and I should not harm him. Also, as his host, I should be protecting his from a murderer, not bearing the knife myself. Besides all of this, Duncan is so meek, and has been so great as king, that his good points will plead like angels blaring trumpets against the sin of his killing. And pity, like a naked new born baby, will stride before the trumpet's blast on unseen horses to deliver the news of his murder to everyone, causing so many tears that they could drown the wind. I have no courage to carry out my intent, I have only great ambition, which can jump over itself and bring me to a fall.

Hey there! What's the news?

He is almost done with his dinner. Why have you left the dining room?

27

MACBETH
Hath he ask'd for me?

Has he asked for me?

LADY MACBETH
Know you not he has?

Don't you know he has?

MACBETH
We will proceed no further in this business:
He hath honour'd me of late; and I have bought
Golden opinions from all sorts of people,
Which would be worn now in their newest gloss,
Not cast aside so soon.

We will go no further in this business.
He has given me great honors recently
and I have won high opinion from all sorts of
people. I should savor this all while it is fresh,
and not cast it aside so soon.

LADY MACBETH
Was the hope drunk
Wherein you dress'd yourself? hath it slept since?
And wakes it now, to look so green and pale
At what it did so freely? From this time
 Such I account thy love. Art thou afeard
To be the same in thine own act and valour
As thou art in desire? Wouldst thou have that
Which thou esteem'st the ornament of life,
And live a coward in thine own esteem,
Letting 'I dare not' wait upon 'I would,'
Like the poor cat i' the adage?

Was the hope that you had drunk,
and has it slept it off since? And now it wakes
up and looks so green and pale, to see what it
did so freely? From this time forward, I will
take account of you. Are you afraid to be
what you truly want to be? Would you have
the crown you want so badly within your
reach, but live like a coward in your own eyes,
allowing 'I can not' to be stronger than
'I will,' like the cat in the old saying?

MACBETH
Prithee, peace:
I dare do all that may become a man;
Who dares do more is none.

Please, be quiet.
I dare to do all a man can.
Who dares to do more than that is not a man.

LADY MACBETH
What beast was't, then,
That made you break this enterprise to me?
When you durst do it, then you were a man;
And, to be more than what you were, you would
Be so much more the man. Nor time nor place
Did then adhere, and yet you would make both:
They have made themselves, and that their fitness now
Does unmake you. I have given suck, and know
How tender 'tis to love the babe that milks me:
I would, while it was smiling in my face,
Have pluck'd my nipple from his boneless gums,
And dash'd the brains out, had I so sworn as you
Have done to this.

What beast was it, then that made you tell all
of this to me? When you told me, you were a
man. And if you were to follow through, you
wouldbe so much more the man! Neither
time or place were set then, and yet you were
ready to make it happen. Now, time and place
have arrived and you are not ready and
willing. I have breast-fed, and I know
how tender it is to love the baby that feeds on
me. I would, however, while it was smiling in
my face, pluck my nipple from its toothless
gums and dash its brains out if I had sworn to
do so, as you have sworn to do this.

28

MACBETH
If we should fail?

What if we fail?

LADY MACBETH
We fail!
But screw your courage to the sticking-place,
And we'll not fail. When Duncan is asleep--
Whereto the rather shall his day's hard journey
Soundly invite him--his two chamberlains
Will I with wine and wassail so convince
That memory, the warder of the brain,
Shall be a fume, and the receipt of reason
A limbeck only: when in swinish sleep
Their drenched natures lie as in a death,
What cannot you and I perform upon
The unguarded Duncan? what not put upon
His spongy officers, who shall bear the guilt
Of our great quell?

Then we fail!
But find your courage and set your mind to it
and we will not fail. When Duncan is asleep,
which he will be soundly after the long
journey he made today, I will wine and woo
his two body guards until they lose their
memory and reason. When they are passed out
like pigs— so out of it they might as well be
dead— there is nothing you and I cannot do
to the unguarded Duncan. And then we
can put the blame on them, as if they did it.

MACBETH
Bring forth men-children only;
For thy undaunted mettle should compose
Nothing but males. Will it not be received,
When we have mark'd with blood those sleepy two
Of his own chamber and used their very daggers,
That they have done't?

You should bear male children, only,
because that unwavering courage should be in
nothing but males. Once we have marked
those two guards with the king's blood and
used their daggers to kill him, won't it look
like they have done it?

LADY MACBETH
Who dares receive it other,
As we shall make our griefs and clamour roar
Upon his death?

Who could possibly see it any other way,
once we make our cries of grief and alarm
when we hear of his death?

MACBETH
I am settled, and bend up
Each corporal agent to this terrible feat.
Away, and mock the time with fairest show:
False face must hide what the false heart
doth know.

I am settled with everything in me to make this
terrible thing happen. Let's go, and pass the
time by looking calm and putting on a happy
face to hide what we know we are about to do.

Exeunt

ACT II

Scene I

Court of Macbeth's Castle.

Enter BANQUO, and FLEANCE bearing a torch before him

BANQUO
How goes the night, boy?

How's your night going, boy?

FLEANCE
The moon is down; I have not heard the clock.

The moon has gone down. I have not heard the clock chime.

BANQUO
And she goes down at twelve.

The moon goes down at midnight.

FLEANCE
I take't, 'tis later, sir.

I think it is later than that, sir.

BANQUO
Hold, take my sword.
There's husbandry in heaven;
Their candles are all out. Take thee that too.
A heavy summons lies like lead upon me,
And yet I would not sleep: merciful powers,
Restrain in me the cursed thoughts that nature
Gives way to in repose!

Here, take my sword.
They are being frugal tonight in heaven;
the candles are all out. Take this, too.
have such a need for sleep, it weighs heavy on
me, but I can't sleep. God help me, and keep
me from the nightmares that come with sleep!

Enter MACBETH, and a Servant with a torch

Give me my sword.
Who's there?

Give me back my sword.
Who's there!

MACBETH
A friend.

A friend.

BANQUO
What, sir, not yet at rest? The king's a-bed:
He hath been in unusual pleasure, and
Sent forth great largess to your offices.
This diamond he greets your wife withal,
By the name of most kind hostess; and shut up
In measureless content.

You haven't gone to bed yet, sir? The king
is asleep. He has been in great spirits and
has given so much to your home. He greeted
your wife with a diamond, calling her the most
kind hostess, and went to bed immeasurably
happy.

MACBETH
Being unprepared,
Our will became the servant to defect;

We were not prepared for the visit,
but tried our best to overcome what lacked

Which else should free have wrought.

*and would have been freely available
otherwise.*

BANQUO
All's well.
I dreamt last night of the three weird sisters:
To you they have show'd some truth.

*All is well.
I dreamt last night of the three witches.
What they said to you proved to be true.*

MACBETH
I think not of them:
Yet, when we can entreat an hour to serve,
We would spend it in some words upon that
business,
If you would grant the time.

*I don't think about them.
But when we can find an hour to do so,
we should talk some more about all of that,*

if you can find the time.

BANQUO
At your kind'st leisure.

Whenever you get a chance.

MACBETH
If you shall cleave to my consent, when 'tis,
It shall make honour for you.

*If you stick to me,
I will honor you in time.*

BANQUO
So I lose none
In seeking to augment it, but still keep
My bosom franchised and allegiance clear,
I shall be counsell'd.

*As long as I lose nothing in seeking
more honor, and can still keep
my heart and conscious clean,
I'll do whatever you say.*

MACBETH
Good repose the while!

Rest well in the meantime!

BANQUO
Thanks, sir: the like to you!

Thanks, sir—the same to you!

Exeunt BANQUO and FLEANCE

MACBETH
Go bid thy mistress, when my drink is ready,

*Go tell your mistress that when my drink is
ready,*

She strike upon the bell. Get thee to bed.

she should ring the bell. Then go to bed.

Exit Servant

Is this a dagger which I see before me,
The handle toward my hand?
Come, let me clutch thee.

*Is this a dagger I see before me with the
handle pointing toward my hand? Let me hold
it. It is not here, and yet I see it.*

I have thee not, and yet I see thee still.
Art thou not, fatal vision, sensible
To feeling as to sight? or art thou but
A dagger of the mind, a false creation,
Proceeding from the heat-oppressed brain?
I see thee yet, in form as palpable
As this which now I draw.
Thou marshall'st me the way that I was going;
And such an instrument I was to use.
Mine eyes are made the fools o' the other senses,
Or else worth all the rest; I see thee still,
And on thy blade and dudgeon gouts of blood,
Which was not so before. There's no such thing:
It is the bloody business which informs
Thus to mine eyes. Now o'er the one halfworld
Nature seems dead, and wicked dreams abuse
The curtain'd sleep; witchcraft celebrates
Pale Hecate's offerings, and wither'd murder,
Alarum'd by his sentinel, the wolf,
Whose howl's his watch,
thus with his stealthy pace.
With Tarquin's ravishing strides, towards his design
Moves like a ghost. Thou sure and firm-set earth,
Hear not my steps, which way they walk, for fear
Thy very stones prate of my whereabout,
And take the present horror from the time,
Which now suits with it. Whiles I threat, he lives:
Words to the heat of deeds too cold breath gives.

A bell rings

I go, and it is done; the bell invites me.
Hear it not, Duncan; for it is a knell
That summons thee to heaven or to hell.

Exit

Is it possible to touch you, dagger, as well as see you? Or are you just a hallucination, a false vison coming from a fever in my brain? You look as real as this dagger I have here. You are guiding me to the place that I was going, and you are like the dagger I was going to use. My eyes are either not working as well as the rest of my senses, or they work better than them all. I still see you, and on your blade and handles I see drops of blood which were not there before. There's no such thing: it is the brutal act I am about to do that causes me see these things. The night world is dark now and nightmares are haunting sleep. Witches are making blood sacrifices, and thin ghost-like murder is awoken by his wolf's cries. Murder strides toward his target like Tarquin, as silently as a ghost. Firm and certain earth beneath my feet—pay no attention to my steps or the way I walk. I fear the stones beneath my feet will reveal where I am going and make the time less perfect for the murder to occur. While I stand here talking, and the talking lessens my resolve to act.

I might as well go and do it. The bell is inviting me to do so. Don't listen to the bell, Duncan. It is summoning you to heaven or to hell.

Scene II

The Same

Enter LADY MACBETH

LADY MACBETH
That which hath made them drunk hath made me bold;
What hath quench'd them hath given me fire.

Hark! Peace!
It was the owl that shriek'd, the fatal bellman,
Which gives the stern'st good-night. He is about it:
The doors are open; and the surfeited grooms
Do mock their charge with snores: I have drugg'd their possets,
That death and nature do contend about them,
Whether they live or die.

*What has made them drunk has made me bold,
and what have quenched them has put me on fire.
Listen! Quiet!
I heard an owl shriek like a bellman delivering a message of death. Macbeth is doing the deed: the doors to the chamber are open and the drunken guards are snoring so loudly it makes their job
a joke. I put so many drugs in their drinks that they sleep as if they are dead.*

MACBETH
[Within] Who's there? what, ho!

[Inside] Who's there? What is that?

LADY MACBETH
Alack, I am afraid they have awaked,
And 'tis not done. The attempt and not the deed
Confounds us. Hark! I laid their daggers ready;
He could not miss 'em. Had he not resembled
My father as he slept, I had done't.

Oh no, I'm afraid the guards have woken up and the murder has not been completed! If we were to get caught in the attempt, it would ruin us. Listen! I put their daggers where Macbeth could easily find them. Had he not looked so much like my father sleeping, I would have killed the king myself.

Enter MACBETH

My husband!

My husband!

MACBETH
I have done the deed. Didst thou not hear a noise?

I have done the deed. Did you hear a noise?

LADY MACBETH
I heard the owl scream and the crickets cry.
Did not you speak?

I heard an owl shriek and I heard the crickets chirp. Didn't you say something?

MACBETH
When?

When?

LADY MACBETH
Now.

Just now.

MACBETH
As I descended?

As I came downstairs?

LADY MACBETH
Ay.

Yes.

MACBETH
Hark!
Who lies i' the second chamber?

Listen to that!
Who is in the other bedroom?

LADY MACBETH
Donalbain.

Donalbain.

MACBETH
This is a sorry sight.

This is a sorry sight.

Looking on his hands

LADY MACBETH
A foolish thought, to say a sorry sight.

That's a foolish thing to say, 'a sorry sight.'

MACBETH
There's one did laugh in's sleep, and one cried
'Murder!'
That they did wake each other:
I stood and heard them:
But they did say their prayers, and address'd them
Again to sleep.

One of the guards laughed in his sleep, and
the other cried 'Murder!' They woke each
other up.
I stood and listened to them. But they said
their prayers
and went back to sleep.

LADY MACBETH
There are two lodged together.

There are two sleeping in the same room.

MACBETH
One cried 'God bless us!' and 'Amen' the other;

As they had seen me with these hangman's hands.
Listening their fear, I could not say 'Amen,'

When they did say 'God bless us!'

One cried 'God bless us!' and the other cried
'Amen.'
It was as if they had seen my bloody hands.
When I heard their fear, I could not say
'Amen'
when they said 'God bless us.'

LADY MACBETH
Consider it not so deeply.

Don't think about it too much.

MACBETH

But wherefore could not I pronounce 'Amen'?
I had most need of blessing, and 'Amen'
Stuck in my throat.

But why couldn't I say 'Amen?'
I was more in need of blessing than ever
but the word 'Amen' stuck in my throat.

LADY MACBETH

These deeds must not be thought
After these ways; so, it will make us mad.

We must not think about all of this so much.
It will make us crazy.

MACBETH

Methought I heard a voice cry 'Sleep no more!
Macbeth does murder sleep', the innocent sleep,
Sleep that knits up the ravell'd sleeve of care,
The death of each day's life, sore labour's bath,
Balm of hurt minds, great nature's second course,
Chief nourisher in life's feast,--

I thought I heard a voice cry out 'Wake up!
Macbeth does murder sleep!' Innocent sleep,
that takes all cares away. The rest at the end
of the day, respite from hard work, peace
for worried minds, the part of the day's feast,
which nourishes us so we may live—

LADY MACBETH

What do you mean?

What are you saying?

MACBETH

Still it cried 'Sleep no more!' to all the house:

The voice kept crying out 'Sleep no more!' to
the whole house.

'Glamis hath murder'd sleep, and therefore Cawdor

'Glamis has killed sleep and so Cawdor will
not be able

Shall sleep no more; Macbeth shall sleep no more.'

to sleep. Macbeth will not be able to sleep.'

LADY MACBETH

Who was it that thus cried? Why, worthy thane,
You do unbend your noble strength, to think
So brainsickly of things. Go get some water,
And wash this filthy witness from your hand.
Why did you bring these daggers from the place?
They must lie there: go carry them; and smear
The sleepy grooms with blood.

Who was it that said all of this? Why, my good
thane, do you weaken yourself by thinking of
such crazy things? Go get some water and
wash the blood from your hands. Why did you
bring these daggers   with you? They have to
stay in the room. Take them back and smear
Duncan's blood over the sleeping guards.

MACBETH

I'll go no more:
I am afraid to think what I have done;
Look on't again I dare not.

I can't go back in there.
I am afraid to think about what I have done
let alone look at it again.

LADY MACBETH

Infirm of purpose!
Give me the daggers: the sleeping and the dead
Are but as pictures: 'tis the eye of childhood
That fears a painted devil. If he do bleed,

You coward! Give me the daggers.
The sleeping and the dead are like pictures.
Only a child would be afraid of such things.
If Duncan is bleeding, I'll paint the faces

I'll gild the faces of the grooms withal;
For it must seem their guilt.

Exit. Knocking within

MACBETH
Whence is that knocking?
How is't with me, when every noise appals me?

What hands are here? ha! they pluck out mine eyes.

Will all great Neptune's ocean wash this blood

Clean from my hand? No, this my hand will rather
The multitudinous seas in incarnadine,
Making the green one red.

Re-enter LADY MACBETH

LADY MACBETH
My hands are of your colour; but I shame
To wear a heart so white.

Knocking within

I hear a knocking
At the south entry: retire we to our chamber;
A little water clears us of this deed:
How easy is it, then! Your constancy
Hath left you unattended.

Knocking within

Hark! more knocking.
Get on your nightgown, lest occasion call us,
And show us to be watchers. Be not lost
So poorly in your thoughts.

MACBETH
To know my deed, 'twere best not know myself.

Knocking within

Wake Duncan with thy knocking!
thou couldst!
Exeunt

of the guards with his blood so they will look guilty.

Where's that knocking coming from? Why is it that every noise is making me so nervous?

Whose hands are these? They make my eyes hurt,
looking at them. Could all of the water in the oceans
wash this blood from my hands? No, it won't. The blood on my hands would turn the green seas to red.

My hands are the same color as yours, but I would be ashamed of myself to have such a weak heart.

I hear knocking at the south entrance. Let's go to our bedroom. A little water will clean off this blood. The rest of this is easy! Your resolve has left you.

Listen! More knocking.
Get into your pajamas in case someone sees that we are awake. Snap out of it! You are lost in a daze!

Knowing what I have done, I wish I did not know myself.

Wake Duncan with your knocking! I would I would if I could.

Scene III

The Same

Knocking within. Enter a Porter

Porter
Here's a knocking indeed! If a
man were porter of hell-gate, he should have
old turning the key.

This is a lot of knocking! If a man were the keeper of hell's gate, he would grow old opening the door so often.

Knocking within

Knock,
knock, knock! Who's there, i' the name of
Beelzebub? Here's a farmer, that hanged
himself on the expectation of plenty: come in
time; have napkins enow about you; here
you'll sweat for't.

*Knock,
knock, knock. Who in the Devil's name is there? It's a famer who hanged himself when the crops did not grow. Come in, and have plenty of napkins on you because you'll be sweating a lot.*

Knocking within

Knock,
knock! Who's there, in the other devil's
name? Faith, here's an equivocator, that could
swear in both the scales against either scale;
who committed treason enough for God's sake,
yet could not equivocate to heaven: O, come
in, equivocator.

Knock, knock, knock. Who's there, in the other devil's name? Oh, it's a smooth talking man who committed treason in God's name, yet could not smooth talk his way into heaven. Come on in, smooth talker.

Knocking within

Knock,
knock, knock! Who's there? Faith, here's an
English tailor come hither, for stealing out of
a French hose: come in, tailor; here you may
roast your goose.

*Knock,
knock, knock! Who's there? I believe it's an English tailor who didn't put enough fabric into a pair of French hose. Come in, tailor— it's hot enough to roast your goose in here!*

Knocking within

Knock,
knock; never at quiet! What are you? But
this place is too cold for hell. I'll devil-porter
it no further: I had thought to have let in
some of all professions that go the primrose
way to the everlasting bonfire.

*Knock,
knock—it's never quiet! What are you? But this place is too cold to be hell. I won't be the devil-porter any longer. I had it in mind to let in some all of the professions that eventually go to hell.*

Knocking within

Anon, anon! I pray you, remember the porter.

I'm coming, I'm coming! Please be good to the porter.

Opens the gate

Enter MACDUFF and LENNOX

MACDUFF
Was it so late, friend, ere you went to bed,
That you do lie so late?

Did you go to be so late, friend, that you decided to sleep in?

Porter
'Faith sir, we were carousing till the
second cock: and drink, sir, is a great
provoker of three things.

It's true, sir, we were partying until three in the morning, and drink, sir, causes three things.

MACDUFF
What three things does drink especially provoke?

What three things does drink cause?

Porter
Marry, sir, nose-painting, sleep, and
urine. Lechery, sir, it provokes, and unprovokes;
it provokes the desire, but it takes
away the performance: therefore, much drink
may be said to be an equivocator with lechery:
it makes him, and it mars him; it sets
him on, and it takes him off; it persuades him,
and disheartens him; makes him stand to, and
not stand to; in conclusion, equivocates him
in a sleep, and, giving him the lie, leaves him.

Well, sir, it causes the nose to turn red and it makes one sleep and urinate a lot. It causes lust, but it takes away lust, as well. meaning, it causes one to feel lustful but takes away the ability to do anything about it. Lots of drinking makes a man feel lustful, but it renders him useless, in this regard. It turns his on, and it turns him off. It makes him have an erection, but the erection does not stay. Drink makes a man dream of having sex, but then drink knocks the man down, and the dream leaves.

MACDUFF
I believe drink gave thee the lie last night.

I believe drink knocked you down last night.

Porter
That it did, sir, i' the very throat on
me: but I requited him for his lie; and, I
think, being too strong for him, though he took
up my legs sometime, yet I made a shift to cast
him.

That it did, sir. Drink got me in the very throat. But I got back at him for knocking me down. I was too strong for him. Although he made my legs unsteady, I vomited him up again.

MACDUFF
Is thy master stirring?

Is Macbeth awake?

Enter MACBETH

Our knocking has awaked him; here he comes.

Our knocking woke him up; here he comes.

LENNOX
Good morrow, noble sir.

Good morning, noble sir!

MACBETH
Good morrow, both.

Good morning to both of you!

MACDUFF
Is the king stirring, worthy thane?

Is the king awake yet, worthy thane?

MACBETH
Not yet.

Not yet.

MACDUFF
He did command me to call timely on him:

I have almost slipp'd the hour.

He commanded me to wake him up early.
I almost missed the hour he wanted me here.

MACBETH
I'll bring you to him.

I'll take you to him.

MACDUFF
I know this is a joyful trouble to you;
But yet 'tis one.

I know this is a joyful trouble to you
to have him here, but trouble all the same.

MACBETH
The labour we delight in physics pain.
This is the door.

The effort we enjoy overcomes the pain.
Here is the door.

MACDUFF
I'll make so bold to call,
For 'tis my limited service.

I will go in and wake him,
since it is my job to do so.

Exit

LENNOX
Goes the king hence to-day?

Does the king leave today?

MACBETH
He does: he did appoint so.

He does, that is what he planned.

LENNOX

The night has been unruly: where we lay,
Our chimneys were blown down;
and, as they say,
Lamentings heard i' the air;
strange screams of death,
And prophesying with accents terrible
Of dire combustion and confused events
New hatch'd to the woeful time:
the obscure bird
Clamour'd the livelong night:
some say, the earth
Was feverous and did shake.

The night has been stormy; where we slept
our chimneys were blown down
and people are saying
they heard laments and cries in the night, and strange
screams of death,
and voices speaking in other languages
predicting terrible events
and a sad time to come.

The veiled bird called out all night long:
some say the earth
was feverish and trembled.

MACBETH

'Twas a rough night.

It was a rough night.

LENNOX

My young remembrance cannot parallel
A fellow to it.

In my short lifetime I cannot remember
another like it.

Re-enter MACDUFF

MACDUFF

O horror, horror, horror! Tongue nor heart
Cannot conceive nor name thee!

Oh, horror, horror, horror! There are no words
to describe the unbelievable thing I have just seen!

MACBETH LENNOX

What's the matter.

What's the matter?

MACDUFF

Confusion now hath made his masterpiece!
Most sacrilegious murder hath broke ope
The Lord's anointed temple,
and stole thence
The life o' the building!

Confusion has created his masterpiece!
A sacrilegious murderer has broken
into the temple and has stolen its life!

MACBETH

What is 't you say? the life?

What are you saying? What do you mean, 'the life?'

LENNOX

Mean you his majesty?

Do you mean the king?

MACDUFF

Approach the chamber,
and destroy your sight

Go into the bedroom
and witness the awful sight yourselves.

With a new Gorgon: do not bid me speak;
See, and then speak yourselves.

What is there will make you freeze in horror.
Do not ask me to describe it.
Go and see for yourselves and then you can
describe it.

Exeunt MACBETH and LENNOX

Awake, awake!
Ring the alarum-bell. Murder and treason!
Banquo and Donalbain! Malcolm! awake!
Shake off this downy sleep, death's counterfeit,
And look on death itself! up, up, and see
The great doom's image! Malcolm! Banquo!
As from your graves rise up, and walk like sprites,

To countenance this horror! Ring the bell.

Wake up! Wake up!
Murder and treason!
Banquo and Donalbain! Malcolm! Wake up!
Shake off your sleep that is like death,
Shake off your sleep that is like death,
and see the face of death! Malcolm! Banquo!
Get out of your grave-like beds and walk like
spirits
to witness this horror. Ring the bell.

Bell rings

Enter LADY MACBETH

LADY MACBETH
What's the business,
That such a hideous trumpet calls to parley
The sleepers of the house? speak, speak!

What's going on? What causes that hideous
trumpet to wake the sleepers of the house?
Speak! Tell me!

MACDUFF
O gentle lady,
'Tis not for you to hear what I can speak:
The repetition, in a woman's ear,
Would murder as it fell.

Oh, gentle lady, it is not for you to hear
what I cannot speak. To repeat it, in a
woman's ear,
would kill as the words were spoken.

Enter BANQUO

O Banquo, Banquo,
Our royal master 's murder'd!

Oh, Banquo, Banquo,
Our royal master has been murdered!

LADY MACBETH
Woe, alas!
What, in our house?

Oh, no! How awful!
Here, in our house?

BANQUO
Too cruel any where.

Dear Duff, I prithee, contradict thyself,
And say it is not so.

It would be too cruel no matter where it
happened.
Dear Duff, please, say you are lying.
Say it is not so.

Re-enter MACBETH and LENNOX, with ROSS

MACBETH

Had I but died an hour before this chance,	*If I had died just an hour before this happened,*
I had lived a blessed time;	*I would have had a blessed life.*
for, from this instant,	*But from this moment on,*
There 's nothing serious in mortality:	*there's nothing serious that makes life worthwhile.*
All is but toys: renown and grace is dead;	*Everything is of little importance: the famous and king is dead.*
The wine of life is drawn, and the mere lees	*The wine of life has been poured, and all that*
Is left this vault to brag of.	*is left in the barrel to speak of is dregs.*

Enter MALCOLM and DONALBAIN

DONALBAIN

What is amiss?	*What's wrong here?*

MACBETH

You are, and do not know't:	*You are, and do not know it:*
The spring, the head,	*the spring, the head,*
the fountain of your blood	*the fountain of your blood*
Is stopp'd; the very source of it is stopp'd.	*has stopped. The very source of it has stopped.*

MACDUFF

Your royal father 's murder'd.	*Your royal father has been murdered.*

MALCOLM

O, by whom?	*Oh? Who did it?*

LENNOX

Those of his chamber,	*The guards of his bedroom,*
as it seem'd, had done 't:	*it seems, have done it.*
Their hands and faces were an badged with blood;	*Their hands and faces were marked with blood.*
So were their daggers, which unwiped we found	*So were their daggers, which we found, un-wiped,*
Upon their pillows:	*upon their pillows: they stared at us, distracted.*
They stared, and were distracted; no man's life	*No man's life was to be trusted with them.*
Was to be trusted with them.	

MACBETH

O, yet I do repent me of my fury, That I did kill them.	*I regret now that I was so furious I killed them.*

MACDUFF
Wherefore did you so?

Why did you go and do that?

MACBETH
Who can be wise, amazed, temperate and furious,
Loyal and neutral, in a moment? No man:
The expedition my violent love
Outrun the pauser, reason. Here lay Duncan,
His silver skin laced with his golden blood;
And his gash'd stabs look'd like a breach in nature
For ruin's wasteful entrance: there, the murderers,
Steep'd in the colours of their trade, their daggers
Unmannerly breech'd with gore: who could refrain,
That had a heart to love, and in that heart
Courage to make 's love known?

Who can be wise, shocked, fair and furious, loyal and neutral, all at the same time? No man can: my violent reaction was born out of love and it outran my reason. There lay Duncan, his white skin covered with his royal blood, and the gashes stabbed in him looked like a sin against nature, allowing for death to make such a wasteful entry. There were the murderers, steeped in the guilt of their act, with their discourteous daggers covered with blood. Who that loved Duncan could keep himself from doing what I did?

LADY MACBETH
Help me hence, ho!

Help me out of here now!

MACDUFF
Look to the lady.

Take care of the lady.

MALCOLM
[Aside to DONALBAIN]
Why do we hold our tongues,
That most may claim this argument for ours?

[Aside to DONALBAIN]
Why are we not saying anything
when we could say so much, being his sons?

DONALBAIN
[Aside to MALCOLM]
What should be spoken here,
where our fate,
Hid in an auger-hole, may rush, and seize us?
Let 's away;
Our tears are not yet brew'd.

[Aside to MALCOLM]
What could we say here,
where our fate, hidden in a drilled hole,
could rush out at any moment and seize us?
Let's get out of here.
We are not ready to cry yet.

MALCOLM
[Aside to DONALBAIN]
Nor our strong sorrow
Upon the foot of motion.

[Aside to DONALBAIN]
And we are not ready
to put our strong sorrow into action yet.

BANQUO
Look to the lady:

Take care of the lady.

LADY MACBETH is carried out

And when we have our naked frailties hid,

When we have dressed for the day let's meet

That suffer in exposure, let us meet,
And question this most bloody piece of work,
To know it further. Fears and scruples shake us:
In the great hand of God I stand; and thence
Against the undivulged pretence I fight
Of treasonous malice.

and try to figure out this murderous act so that we may understand what happened. We are shaken by fear and doubt. By God's hand I plan to fight against this secret plot of treason and malice.

MACDUFF
And so do I.

I do, too.

ALL
So all.

We all do.

MACBETH
Let's briefly put on manly readiness,
And meet i' the hall together.

Let's get properly dressed and meet in the hall together.

ALL
Well contented.

That sounds good.

Exeunt all but Malcolm and Donalbain.

MALCOLM
What will you do? Let's not consort with them:
To show an unfelt sorrow is an office
Which the false man does easy. I'll to England.

What are you going to do? Let's not meet with them. It's easy to show sorrow you don't really feel if you are a liar. I'll go to England.

DONALBAIN
To Ireland, I; our separated fortune
Shall keep us both the safer: where we are,
There's daggers in men's smiles: the near in blood,
The nearer bloody.

I'll go to Ireland. We will have better luck of staying safe if we separate. There are daggers in men's smiles here. Our relatives are the most likely to kill us.

MALCOLM
This murderous shaft that's shot
Hath not yet lighted, and our safest way
Is to avoid the aim. Therefore, to horse;
And let us not be dainty of leave-taking,
But shift away: there's warrant in that theft
Which steals itself, when there's no mercy left.

We may be in harm's way, but it has not found us yet. The safest thing to do it to avoid it. So, let's get on our horses and leave without goodbyes. There's no mercy here, and that is good reason to leave.

Exeunt

Scene IV

Outside Macbeth's Castle

Enter ROSS and an old Man

Old Man
Threescore and ten I can remember well:
Within the volume of which time I have seen
Hours dreadful and things strange;
but this sore night
Hath trifled former knowings.

*I can remember the past seventy years.
In that time, I've seen dreadful times and
strange things,
but this awful night
has made that all seem like nothing.*

ROSS
Ah, good father,
Thou seest, the heavens, as troubled with man's act,
Threaten his bloody stage: by the clock, 'tis day,
And yet dark night strangles the travelling lamp:
Is't night's predominance, or the day's shame,
That darkness does the face of earth entomb,
When living light should kiss it?

*Oh, good father, you can see that the skies are
troubled and threaten the bloody earth. It is
day, but darkness, like the night, strangles the
sun. Is it because night is stronger, or because
the day is so full of shame that darkness
overtakes the earth when the light of day
should bless it?*

Old Man
'Tis unnatural,
Even like the deed that's done. On Tuesday last,
A falcon, towering in her pride of place,

Was by a mousing owl hawk'd at and kill'd.

*It's unnatural, just like the murder that has
taken place. Last Tuesday a falcon, circling in
the sky with pride, was killed by a hawk that
usually only goes after mice.*

ROSS
And Duncan's horses--a thing most strange
and certain--
Beauteous and swift, the minions of their race,
Turn'd wild in nature, broke their stalls, flung out,
Contending 'gainst obedience, as they would make
War with mankind.

*Did you hear that Duncan's horses, beautiful
and swift—the best
of their kind—broke out of their stalls and
went wild, refusing to obey anyone, as if they
were are war with mankind.
Isn't that strange?*

Old Man
'Tis said they eat each other.

People say they ate each other.

ROSS
They did so, to the amazement of mine eyes
That look'd upon't. Here comes the good Macduff.

*They did. I saw it and it amazed me.
Here comes the good Macduff.*

Enter MACDUFF

46

How goes the world, sir, now?

How are things going, sir?

MACDUFF
Why, see you not?

Can't you see for yourself?

ROSS
Is't known who did this more than bloody deed?

Do they know who committed the murder?

MACDUFF
Those that Macbeth hath slain.

The men who Macbeth killed did it.

ROSS
Alas, the day!
What good could they pretend?

It's sad he killed them.
Why would they have done it?

MACDUFF
They were suborn'd:
Malcolm and Donalbain, the king's two sons,
Are stol'n away and fled; which puts upon them
Suspicion of the deed.

They were paid to do it.
Malcolm and Donalbain, the king's sons, have
snuck away and fled. That puts the suspicion
on them.

ROSS
'Gainst nature still!
Thriftless ambition, that wilt ravin up

Thine own life's means! Then 'tis most like
The sovereignty will fall upon Macbeth.

That's so against nature!
What sort of extravagant ambition would
cause them
to do away with the one who provides for
them. So, it looks like Macbeth will become
king.

MACDUFF
He is already named, and gone to Scone
To be invested.

He has already been named, and has gone to
Scone to be crowned.

ROSS
Where is Duncan's body?

Where is Duncan's body?

MACDUFF
Carried to Colmekill,
The sacred storehouse of his predecessors,
And guardian of their bones.

It's been taken to Colmekill to the tomb
of his predecessors.
Their bones are safe there.

ROSS
Will you to Scone?

Will you go to Scone?

MACDUFF
No, cousin, I'll to Fife.

No, cousin, I'm going to Fife.

ROSS

Well, I will thither. *Well, I'll go to Scone.*

MACDUFF

Well, may you see things well done there: adieu! *Well, I hope you will see that things are well done there.*

Lest our old robes sit easier than our new! *Goodbye! I fear that the old ways are easier than the new!*

ROSS

Farewell, father. *Goodbye, father.*

Old Man

God's benison go with you; and with those *May God's blessings go with you, and also with those*

That would make good of bad, and friends of foes! *who would make good of bad, and friends of enemies!*

Exeunt

Act III

Scene I

Forres. The Palace.

Enter BANQUO

BANQUO
Thou hast it now: king, Cawdor, Glamis, all,
As the weird women promised, and, I fear,
Thou play'dst most foully for't: yet it was said
It should not stand in thy posterity,
But that myself should be the root and father
Of many kings. If there come truth from them--
As upon thee, Macbeth, their speeches shine--
Why, by the verities on thee made good,
May they not be my oracles as well,
And set me up in hope? But hush! no more.

You have it all now: king, Cawdor, Glamis, all. Just like the witches promised. I'm afraid you engaged in foul play for it. Still, it was said that the line would not be passed down to your children, but that I will be the father of many kings. If the witches tell the truth—as they seemed to have done with you—well, perhaps what they said about me will come true, as well. Perhaps they can see my future, too, and give me hope? But, shhhh. I should say no more.

Sennet sounded. Enter MACBETH, as king, LADY MACBETH, as queen, LENNOX, ROSS, Lords, Ladies, and Attendants

MACBETH
Here's our chief guest.

Here's our main guest.

LADY MACBETH
If he had been forgotten,
It had been as a gap in our great feast,
And all-thing unbecoming.

*If he had been forgotten,
it would have made a gap in our big
celebration and would not be in line with our
standards.*

MACBETH
To-night we hold a solemn supper sir,
And I'll request your presence.

*Tonight we hold a solemn celebration, sir,
and I request your presence.*

BANQUO
Let your highness
Command upon me; to the which my duties
Are with a most indissoluble tie
For ever knit.

*Anything you command, my highness,
I am bound to do.*

MACBETH
Ride you this afternoon?

Are you going riding this afternoon?

BANQUO
Ay, my good lord.

Yes, my good lord.

MACBETH
We should have else desired your good advice,
Which still hath been both grave and prosperous,
In this day's council; but we'll take to-morrow.
Is't far you ride?

We would have liked to hear your advice, which has always been both serious and successful, in today's council, but we can hear it tomorrow. Are you riding far?

BANQUO
As far, my lord, as will fill up the time
'Twixt this and supper: go not my horse the better,
I must become a borrower of the night
For a dark hour or twain.

I'm going to ride as far as it will take between now and supper. Unless my horse goes faster than I expect, I will be back an hour or two after dark.

MACBETH
Fail not our feast.

Don't miss our feast.

BANQUO
My lord, I will not.

My lord, I will not miss it.

MACBETH
We hear, our bloody cousins are bestow'd
In England and in Ireland, not confessing
Their cruel parricide, filling their hearers
With strange invention: but of that to-morrow,
When therewithal we shall have cause of state
Craving us jointly. Hie you to horse: adieu,
Till you return at night. Goes Fleance with you?

We hear our murderous cousins are stowed away in England and in Ireland, not confessing to cruelly killing their father. They tell all who listen terrible lies. But we'll talk more about that tomorrow, when we talk about matters of the state that concern us both. Go to your horse: goodbye until you return tonight. Is Fleance going with you?

BANQUO
Ay, my good lord: our time does call upon 's.

Yes, my good lord. It's time we leave.

MACBETH
I wish your horses swift and sure of foot;
And so I do commend you to their backs.
Farewell.

I hope your horses are swift and sure of foot. And with that, you should go to them. Farewell.

Exit BANQUO

Let every man be master of his time
Till seven at night: to make society
The sweeter welcome, we will keep ourself
Till supper-time alone: while then,
God be with you!

Let every man do want he wants to do until seven tonight: to make your company all the better, I will keep to myself until supper time. So, then, God be with you!

Exeunt all but MACBETH, and an attendant

Sirrah, a word with you: attend those men

You, there, can you tell me:

Our pleasure?

are those men waiting for me?

ATTENDANT
They are, my lord, without the palace gate.

They are, my lord, outside the palace gate.

MACBETH
Bring them before us.

Bring them to me.

Exit Attendant

To be thus is nothing;
But to be safely thus.--Our fears in Banquo
Stick deep; and in his royalty of nature
Reigns that which would be fear'd:
'tis much he dares;
And, to that dauntless temper of his mind,
He hath a wisdom that doth guide his valour
To act in safety. There is none but he
Whose being I do fear: and, under him,
My Genius is rebuked; as, it is said,
Mark Antony's was by Caesar. He chid the sisters
When first they put the name of king upon me,
And bade them speak to him: then prophet-like
They hail'd him father to a line of kings:
Upon my head they placed a fruitless crown,
And put a barren sceptre in my gripe,
Thence to be wrench'd with an unlineal hand,
No son of mine succeeding. If 't be so,
For Banquo's issue have I filed my mind;
For them the gracious Duncan have I murder'd;
Put rancours in the vessel of my peace
Only for them; and mine eternal jewel
Given to the common enemy of man,
To make them kings, the seed of Banquo kings!
Rather than so, come fate into the list.
And champion me to the utterance! Who's there!

To be king is nothing if I am not safe.
I fear Banquo deeply; there's something regal
in his nature that should be feared. He is bold,
and his mind is fearless and active. He has the
wisdom to guide his bravery. There is no one
but him that I fear, and under him, my
guardian spirit is rebuked, as they say Mark
Anthony's was by Caesar. He scolded the
witches when they first said that I would be
king, and asked them to speak to him Then,
like prophets, they said he would be father
to a line of kings: on my head they placed a
fruitless crown and put a scepter in my hand I
can't pass down. These will be taken by
someone outside the family since I will not
have a son. If this is how it is, then it's for
Banquo's sons I've worried my mind
and murdered the gracious Duncan.
I've disturbed my own peace for them,
and have given my eternal life to the devil
to make them kings, the seed of Banquo,
kings! Instead of watching this happen, I will
enlist fate to battle, and will fight until my last
breath. Who's there!

Re-enter Attendant, with two Murderers

Now go to the door, and stay there till we call.

Now go to the door and stay there until I call you.

Exit Attendant

Was it not yesterday we spoke together?

Wasn't it just yesterday we talked?

52

First Murderer

It was, so please your highness.

It was, you are right, your highness.

MACBETH

Well then, now
Have you consider'd of my speeches? Know
That it was he in the times past which held you
So under fortune, which you thought had been
Our innocent self: this I made good to you
In our last conference, pass'd in probation with you,
How you were borne in hand, how cross'd,
the instruments,
Who wrought with them, and all things else that
might
To half a soul and to a notion crazed
Say 'Thus did Banquo.'

*Well, have you thought about what I said?
You know that it was him who held you back
and brought you bad luck, even though you
thought it was me, but I was innocent. I made
this clear to you during our last meeting and
proved it to you. I showed you how you were
deluded and crossed. I showed you the papers
he used to do these things, and all sorts of
other things that would convince
even someone with half a soul and who is
crazy to say 'It was Banquo who did this.'*

First Murderer

You made it known to us.

You made it clear to us.

MACBETH

I did so, and went further, which is now
Our point of second meeting. Do you find
Your patience so predominant in your nature
That you can let this go? Are you so gospell'd
To pray for this good man and for his issue,
Whose heavy hand hath bow'd you to the grave
And beggar'd yours for ever?

*I did, and I went even further, which is the
point of this second meeting. Are you such
patient men that you can let this go? Are you
so forgiving that you will pray for this good
man and his sons, whose heavy hand has
pointed you toward the grave
and made beggars of you and your family
forever?*

First Murderer

We are men, my liege.

We are, my lord.

MACBETH

Ay, in the catalogue ye go for men;
As hounds and greyhounds, mongrels,
spaniels, curs,
Shoughs, water-rugs and demi-wolves, are clept

All by the name of dogs: the valued file
Distinguishes the swift, the slow, the subtle,
The housekeeper, the hunter, every one
According to the gift which bounteous nature
Hath in him closed; whereby he does receive
Particular addition. from the bill
That writes them all alike: and so of men.

*Yes, you are part of the species known as man,
just like hounds and greyhounds, mongrels,
spaniels, mutts,
shaggy dogs, English rough water dogs and
wolf-dog hybrids
are all known as dogs. But a list of dogs will
distinguish which ones are fast, or slow, or
clever, or watchdogs, which are hunters—
every dog is classified according to the gift
nature has given him, and he receives
particular distinction from the rest of the list
that only describes the ways they are alike.*

Now, if you have a station in the file,
Not i' the worst rank of manhood, say 't;
And I will put that business in your bosoms,
Whose execution takes your enemy off,
Grapples you to the heart and love of us,
Who wear our health but sickly in his life,
Which in his death were perfect.

It's the same with men.
So, if you have a place among men that isn't
in the worst rank, tell me. I will assign you the
business that, carried out, will rid you of your
enemy. It will bring you closer to me, and to
special attention from me. If Banquo were
dead, my health would be perfect.

Second Murderer
I am one, my liege,
Whom the vile blows and buffets of the world
Have so incensed that I am reckless what
I do to spite the world.

My lord,
I'm so angry at the way the world has
beaten me that I would do anything to get
back.

First Murderer
And I another
So weary with disasters, tugg'd with fortune,
That I would set my lie on any chance,
To mend it, or be rid on't.

Me, too.
I'm so tired of the bad luck and disasters,
that I would jump on any chance to be rid of
it, or die.

MACBETH
Both of you
Know Banquo was your enemy.

Both of you know that Banquo was your
enemy.

Both Murderers
True, my lord.

Yes, my lord.

MACBETH
So is he mine; and in such bloody distance,
That every minute of his being thrusts
Against my near'st of life: and though I could
With barefaced power sweep him from my sight
And bid my will avouch it, yet I must not,
For certain friends that are both his and mine,
Whose loves I may not drop, but wail his fall
Who I myself struck down; and thence it is,
That I to your assistance do make love,
Masking the business from the common eye
For sundry weighty reasons.

He is my enemy, too, and I hate him so much
that every minute he lives thrusts against my
heart. Even though I have the power to sweep
him away and my word can kill him, I must
not do that because we have some friends in
common who I don't want to lose, and I would
need to grieve his death, even though it was
me who had him killed. So, because of that, I
need your help and am asking
you to do this so that no one knows who killed
Banquo.

Second Murderer
We shall, my lord,
Perform what you command us.

We will do
what you command us, my lord.

First Murderer
Though our lives—

Although our lives—

MACBETH
Your spirits shine through you.
Within this hour at most
I will advise you where to plant yourselves;
Acquaint you with the perfect spy o' the time,
The moment on't; for't must be done to-night,
And something from the palace; always thought
That I require a clearness: and with him--
To leave no rubs nor botches in the work--
Fleance his son, that keeps him company,
Whose absence is no less material to me
Than is his father's, must embrace the fate
Of that dark hour. Resolve yourselves apart:
I'll come to you anon.

*Your determination shines through you.
I will tell you within an hour where you
should go and when. It must be done tonight,
and away from the palace. Keep in mind that
no one must suspect me. You must not mess
this up or leave any evidence. His son,
Fleance, will be with him, and he must be
killed, too. I need him gone, as well.
Make up your minds about this. I'll come to
you soon.*

Both Murderers
We are resolved, my lord.

We have made up our minds, my lord.

MACBETH
I'll call upon you straight: abide within.

I'll call for you soon. Wait inside.

Exeunt Murderers

It is concluded. Banquo, thy soul's flight,
If it find heaven, must find it out to-night.

*It is done. Banquo, if your soul is going to
heaven, it will be tonight.*

Exit

Scene II

The Palace

Enter LADY MACBETH and a Servant

LADY MACBETH
Is Banquo gone from court?

Has Banquo left the court?

Servant
Ay, madam, but returns again to-night.

Yes, madam, but he returns tonight.

LADY MACBETH
Say to the king, I would attend his leisure
For a few words.

*Tell the king I would like to talk to him
for a moment.*

Servant
Madam, I will.

I will do that, madam.

Exit

LADY MACBETH
Nought's had, all's spent,
Where our desire is got without content:
'Tis safer to be that which we destroy
Than by destruction dwell in doubtful joy.

*When you've spent everything, but have
nothing, when you've gotten what you
wanted but are not happy, It is better
to be the one who died than to live with
uneasiness.*

Enter MACBETH

How now, my lord! why do you keep alone,
Of sorriest fancies your companions making,
Using those thoughts which should indeed have
died
With them they think on?
Things without all remedy
Should be without regard: what's done is done.

*How are you, my lord! Why are you keeping
Those thoughts should have died with those
you think about*

You shouldn't dwell on what

you cannot change: what's done is done.

MACBETH
We have scotch'd the snake, not kill'd it:
She'll close and be herself, whilst our poor malice
Remains in danger of her former tooth.
But let the frame of things disjoint, both the
worlds suffer,
Ere we will eat our meal in fear and sleep
In the affliction of these terrible dreams
That shake us nightly: better be with the dead,

*We have injured the snake but not killed it.
She will heal and be herself again and we
remain in danger of her fangs. The universe
may fall apart and heaven and earth will
suffer,
and I will eat my meals in fear and sleep
with nightmares shaking me nightly.
We'd be better off with the dead we killed*

Whom we, to gain our peace, have sent to peace,
Than on the torture of the mind to lie
In restless ecstasy. Duncan is in his grave;
After life's fitful fever he sleeps well;
Treason has done his worst: nor steel, nor poison,
Malice domestic, foreign levy, nothing,
Can touch him further.

*in order to gain our peace rather than
suffering this torture of the mind. Duncan is in
his grave. after life's unrest he sleeps well;
The worst that happened to him was treason:
no steel or poison, violence in his country,
foreign war— nothing can touch him now.*

LADY MACBETH
Come on;
Gentle my lord, sleek o'er your rugged looks;
Be bright and jovial among your guests to-night.

*Come on,
relax, my lord. Change your expression.
Be bright and jovial with your guests tonight.*

MACBETH
So shall I, love; and so, I pray, be you:
Let your remembrance apply to Banquo;
Present him eminence, both with eye and tongue:
Unsafe the while, that we
Must lave our honours in these flattering streams,
And make our faces vizards to our hearts,
Disguising what they are.

*I will, my love, and so should you.
Pay special attention to Banquo.
Make him feel superior and important,
with the way you look at him and what you
say. We are in danger and must give him
honor and flatter him, and not allow our
faces to reveal what is in our hearts.*

LADY MACBETH
You must leave this.

You must stop talking like this.

MACBETH
O, full of scorpions is my mind, dear wife!
Thou know'st that Banquo, and his Fleance, lives.

*Oh, my mind is full of scorpions, my dear
wife! You know that Banquo and his son live.*

LADY MACBETH
But in them nature's copy's not eterne.

*But only as long as they live—
they are not eternal.*

MACBETH
There's comfort yet; they are assailable;
Then be thou jocund: ere the bat hath flown
His cloister'd flight, ere to black Hecate's summons
The shard-borne beetle with his drowsy hums
Hath rung night's yawning peal, there shall be done
A deed of dreadful note.

*There's a comforting thought—they can die.
So be lighthearted: before the bat has flown
tonight into the darkness, before night falls
and the scaly-winged beetle has begun his
evening humming to usher out the day,
a terrible thing will happen.*

LADY MACBETH
What's to be done?

What's going to happen?

MACBETH
Be innocent of the knowledge, dearest chuck,
Till thou applaud the deed. Come, seeling night,

*I am not going to tell you, my sweet little
chicken, until you can applaud it. Come,*

Scarf up the tender eye of pitiful day;
And with thy bloody and invisible hand
Cancel and tear to pieces that great bond
Which keeps me pale! Light thickens; and the crow
Makes wing to the rooky wood:
Good things of day begin to droop and drowse;
While night's black agents to their preys do rouse.
Thou marvell'st at my words: but hold thee still;
Things bad begun make strong themselves by ill.
So, prithee, go with me.

Exeunt

until you can applaud it. Come, night, and cover the eye of day. With your bloody and invisible hand, cancel and rip to pieces the bond that keeps me pale! Darkness is falling, and the crow makes its way home to the woods. The good things of the daytime are drooping and falling to sleep, while night's black agents rise to hunt. You wonder at my words, but be still. Once they are started, bad things feed on more bad things. So, please, come with me.

Scene III

A Park Near the Palace

Enter three Murderers

First Murderer
But who did bid thee join with us?

But who told you to join us?

Third Murderer
Macbeth.

Macbeth.

Second Murderer
He needs not our mistrust, since he delivers
Our offices and what we have to do
To the direction just.

There's no need not to trust him since he is here to tell us what we are to do.

First Murderer
Then stand with us.
The west yet glimmers with some streaks of day:
Now spurs the lated traveller apace
To gain the timely inn; and near approaches
The subject of our watch.

Then stay with us. The sky still shows some daylight. Now is the time a late traveler quickens the pace to get to the destination on time. The man we are watching for is getting closer.

Third Murderer
Hark! I hear horses.

Listen! I hear horses.

BANQUO
[Within] Give us a light there, ho!

[Within] Hello! Give us some light here!

Second Murderer
Then 'tis he: the rest
That are within the note of expectation
Already are i' the court.

*This is him.
The rest that are expected tonight are already inside.*

First Murderer
His horses go about.

His horses are walking about.

Third Murderer
Almost a mile: but he does usually,
So all men do, from hence to the palace gate
Make it their walk.

It's almost a mile to the palace gate. But he, like the other men, will walk the horses from here.

Second Murderer
A light, a light!

Give me a light! Give me a light!

Enter BANQUO, and FLEANCE with a torch

Third Murderer
'Tis he.

It's him.

First Murderer
Stand to't.

Let's go to it.

BANQUO
It will be rain to-night.

It's going to rain tonight.

First Murderer
Let it come down.

Let it pour!

They set upon BANQUO

BANQUO
O, treachery! Fly, good Fleance, fly, fly, fly!
Thou mayst revenge. O slave!

Oh, treachery! Run, good Fleance, run, run, run! Avenge my death. Oh, you hired hand!

Dies. FLEANCE escapes

Third Murderer
Who did strike out the light?

Who put out the light?

First Murderer
Wast not the way?

Wasn't that the thing to do?

Third Murderer
There's but one down; the son is fled.

There's only one dead, here. The son has fled.

Second Murderer
We have lost
Best half of our affair.

*We lost
the better half of what we were to do.*

First Murderer
Well, let's away, and say how much is done.

Well, let's get out of here, and tell Macbeth how much we did.

Exeunt

Scene IV

The Same. Hall in the Palace.

A banquet prepared. Enter MACBETH, LADY MACBETH, ROSS, LENNOX, Lords, and Attendants

MACBETH
You know your own degrees; sit down: at first
And last the hearty welcome.

You know your titles so you know where to be seated. A hearty welcome to all!

Lords
Thanks to your majesty.

Thank you, your majesty.

MACBETH
Ourself will mingle with society,
And play the humble host.
Our hostess keeps her state, but in best time
We will require her welcome.

I will mingle with you and play the humble host.
Our hostess will stay in her seat, but when the time is right, she will welcome you.

LADY MACBETH
Pronounce it for me, sir, to all our friends;
For my heart speaks they are welcome.

Say it for me, sir, to all of our friends. In my heart they are welcome.

First Murderer appears at the door

MACBETH
See, they encounter thee with their hearts' thanks.
Both sides are even: here I'll sit i' the midst:
Be large in mirth; anon we'll drink a measure
The table round.

And they respond with thanks from their hearts, so both sides are even. Here, I'll sit in the middle: be full of gladness and gaiety. Soon, we'll drink a toast around the table.

Approaching the door

There's blood on thy face.

There's blood on your face.

First Murderer
'Tis Banquo's then.

It's Banquo's then.

MACBETH
'Tis better thee without than he within.
Is he dispatch'd?

It's better on the outside of you instead of inside him. Is he dead?

First Murderer
My lord, his throat is cut; that I did for him.

My lord, his throat is slit. I did it.

MACBETH
Thou art the best o' the cut-throats: yet he's good
That did the like for Fleance: if thou didst it,
Thou art the nonpareil.

You are the best of killers. Yet whoever did the same to Fleance is also good. If you did both of them, you are without equal.

First Murderer
Most royal sir,
Fleance is 'scaped.

Most royal sir,
Fleance has escaped.

MACBETH
Then comes my fit again: I had else been perfect,
Whole as the marble, founded as the rock,
As broad and general as the casing air:
But now I am cabin'd, cribb'd, confined, bound in
To saucy doubts and fears. But Banquo's safe?

My fears come back again. I had been perfect, whole as the marble in the rock and as open and free as the air around it. But now I am bound up and confined with doubts and fears. and confined with doubts and fears. But Banquo's dead, for sure?

First Murderer
Ay, my good lord: safe in a ditch he bides,
With twenty trenched gashes on his head;
The least a death to nature.

Yes, my good lord. He lies dead in a ditch with twenty deep gashes on his head, any which would have killed him.

MACBETH
Thanks for that:
There the grown serpent lies; the worm that's fled
Hath nature that in time will venom breed,
No teeth for the present. Get thee gone: to-morrow
We'll hear, ourselves, again.

Thanks for doing that.
The grown snake is dead, but the younger snake has fled. In time he will become a threat, but not for the time being. Go on, then, tomorrow you'll hear from me again.

Exit Murderer

LADY MACBETH
My royal lord,
You do not give the cheer: the feast is sold
That is not often vouch'd, while 'tis a-making,
'Tis given with welcome:
to feed were best at home;
From thence the sauce to meat is ceremony;
Meeting were bare without it.

My royal lord,
You have not given the toast. The dinner feels taxing without frequent toasts. Toasting makes the guests feel welcome. They may as well be eating at home, since the pleasure of dining out lies in the ritual of toasting. It's not the same without it.

MACBETH
Sweet remembrancer!
Now, good digestion wait on appetite,
And health on both!

It's sweet of you to remind me!
Here's to good digestion after your appetite!
May both be healthy!

LENNOX
May't please your highness sit.

Please, your highness, sit if you'd like.

The GHOST OF BANQUO enters, and sits in MACBETH's place

MACBETH
Here had we now our country's honour roof'd,
Were the graced person of our Banquo present;
Who may I rather challenge for unkindness
Than pity for mischance!

We would have all of our country's nobility here if Banquo graced our presence. I would rather challenge him for being rude than hear that something bad happened to him.

ROSS
His absence, sir,
Lays blame upon his promise.
Please't your highness
To grace us with your royal company.

He's not here because he broke his promise, sir.
Please, your highness, join us.

MACBETH
The table's full.

The table's full.

LENNOX
Here is a place reserved, sir.

Here is a place reserved for you, sir.

MACBETH
Where?

Where?

LENNOX
Here, my good lord.
What is't that moves your highness?

Here, my good lord.
What is wrong, your highess?

MACBETH
Which of you have done this?

Which one of you did this?

Lords
What, my good lord?

Did what, my good lord?

MACBETH
Thou canst not say I did it: never shake
Thy gory locks at me.

You can not say I did it. Do not shake your bloody head at me.

ROSS
Gentlemen, rise: his highness is not well.

Gentlemen, stand up. His highness is not well.

LADY MACBETH
Sit, worthy friends: my lord is often thus,
And hath been from his youth: pray you, keep seat;
The fit is momentary; upon a thought
He will again be well: if much you note him,
You shall offend him and extend his passion:

Sit back down, my good friends. My lord is frequently like this and has been from his youth. Please, stay seated. The fit is temporary, in a moment he will be well again. If you pay too much attention to him, you will

Feed, and regard him not. Are you a man?

MACBETH
Ay, and a bold one, that dare look on that
Which might appal the devil.

LADY MACBETH
O proper stuff!
This is the very painting of your fear:
This is the air-drawn dagger which, you said,
Led you to Duncan. O, these flaws and starts,
Impostors to true fear, would well become
A woman's story at a winter's fire,
Authorized by her grandam. Shame itself!
Why do you make such faces? When all's done,
You look but on a stool.

MACBETH
Prithee, see there! behold! look! lo!
how say you?
Why, what care I? If thou canst nod, speak too.
If charnel-houses and our graves must send
Those that we bury back, our monuments
Shall be the maws of kites.

GHOST OF BANQUO vanishes

LADY MACBETH
What, quite unmann'd in folly?

MACBETH
If I stand here, I saw him.

LADY MACBETH
Fie, for shame!

MACBETH
Blood hath been shed ere now, i' the olden time,
Ere human statute purged the gentle weal;
Ay, and since too, murders have been perform'd
Too terrible for the ear: the times have been,
That, when the brains were out, the man would die,
And there an end; but now they rise again,
With twenty mortal murders on their crowns,
And push us from our stools: this is more strange

offend him and it will last longer. Eat, and pay no attention to him. Are you a man?

Yes, and a brave one that dares to look at something that would shock the devil.

Oh, come on! This is a hallucination created by fear. This is just like the dagger you said you saw in the air—the one that led you to Duncan? These sudden and passionate outbursts of yours are like imposters of true fear. They would be fit for a woman telling a story to her grandmother in front of a winter fire. It is shameful how you act! Why do you have to make such faces? When all is said and done, it's just a stool you are looking at.

Please, look there! Look at that! See it? Look! What do you have to say? And why should I care? If you can nod, speak, too. If our vaults and graves are going to send back those we bury, they will end up in the stomachs of birds.

What, are you undone by this foolishness?

As I stand here, I saw him.

I'm disappointed in you.

In olden times, before laws were made, a lot of blood was shed. And even since then, murders too terrible to mention have been committed. In the past, when you beat a man's brains out, he died, and it was over. But now, they rise again, with twenty fatal wounds when you beat a man's brains out, they rise again, with twenty fatal wounds to the head, and push us out of our seat.

LADY MACBETH
My worthy lord,
Your noble friends do lack you.

MACBETH
I do forget.
Do not muse at me, my most worthy friends,
I have a strange infirmity, which is nothing
To those that know me.
Come, love and health to all;
Then I'll sit down. Give me some wine; fill full.
I drink to the general joy o' the whole table,
And to our dear friend Banquo, whom we miss;
Would he were here! to all, and him, we thirst,
And all to all.

Lords
Our duties, and the pledge.

Re-enter GHOST OF BANQUO

MACBETH
Avaunt! and quit my sight!
let the earth hide thee!
Thy bones are marrowless, thy blood is cold;
Thou hast no speculation in those eyes
Which thou dost glare with!

LADY MACBETH
Think of this, good peers,
But as a thing of custom: 'tis no other;
Only it spoils the pleasure of the time.

MACBETH
What man dare, I dare:
Approach thou like the rugged Russian bear,
The arm'd rhinoceros, or the Hyrcan tiger;
Take any shape but that, and my firm nerves
Shall never tremble: or be alive again,
And dare me to the desert with thy sword;
If trembling I inhabit then, protest me
The baby of a girl. Hence, horrible shadow!
Unreal mockery, hence!

This is much more strange than any murder.

My good lord,
your friends miss your presence.

I forgot about them.
Do not pay much attention to me, my most
worthy friends, I have a strange illness which
is nothing to those who know me well.
Come, let's drink a toast to love and health for
all, then I'll sit down. Give me some wine—
top it up! I drink to the general joy of the
whole table, and to our dear friend Banquo,
who I miss. If only he were here! To all of you
and to him, let's drink. Everybody, drink!

We pledge our best.

Go away!
Leave my sight! Let your grave hold you!
Your bones have no marrow and your blood is
cold.
You have no life in those eyes that you glare at
me with!

Think of this, good friends, as a common
behavior in our house. It is nothing else, but it
spoils the fun we are having.

Whatever man has courage to do, I have
courage to do. You can approach me looking
like a rugged Russian bear, a horned
rhinoceros, or an ancient Asian tiger.
Take any shape but the one you have, and my
firm nerves will not tremble. Come to life
again, and dare me in the desert to a sword
fight. If I show any trembling, then call me a
child's doll. Get out of here, horrible shadow!
Strange imitation, get out of here!

GHOST OF BANQUO vanishes

Why, so: being gone,
I a man again. Pray you, sit still.

Now that it is gone, I am myself again.
Please, stay seated.

LADY MACBETH
You have displaced the mirth,
broke the good meeting,
With most admired disorder.

You have disrupted the fun
and broke up the party
with most amazing confusion.

MACBETH
Can such things be,
And overcome us like a summer's cloud,
Without our special wonder?
You make me strange
Even to the disposition that I owe,
When now I think you can behold such sights,
And keep the natural ruby of your cheeks,
When mine is blanched with fear.

How can such sights overcome us like a cloud
on a sunny day without making us stop on a
sunny day without making us stop and
wonder? You make me feel strange and not
like myself when I see how you can witness
such sights and keep the color in your face,
while mine is white with fear.

ROSS
What sights, my lord?

What sights, my lord?

LADY MACBETH
I pray you, speak not; he grows worse and worse;
Question enrages him. At once, good night:
Stand not upon the order of your going,
But go at once.

I beg you, don't speak to him. He's just
getting worse, and questions will make him
angry. Now, good night. Do not take the
trouble to exit properly, just leave.

LENNOX
Good night; and better health
Attend his majesty!

Good night. I hope his majesty is better soon!

LADY MACBETH
A kind good night to all!

A kind good night to all!

Exeunt all but MACBETH and LADY MACBETH

MACBETH
It will have blood;
they say, blood will have blood:
Stones have been known to move and trees
to speak;
Augurs and understood relations have
By magot-pies and choughs and rooks brought
forth

It will have blood.
They say blood will have blood.
Stones have been known to move and trees to
speak.
Priests and those that understand how to do
so can bring forth a man's guilt using birds
that talk.

The secret'st man of blood. What is the night?

What time of night is it?

LADY MACBETH
Almost at odds with morning, which is which.

It's the middle of the night.

MACBETH
How say'st thou, that Macduff denies his person
At our great bidding?

*What do you think about Macduff refusing
to come when requested?*

LADY MACBETH
Did you send to him, sir?

Did you ask for him, sir?

MACBETH
I hear it by the way; but I will send:
There's not a one of them but in his house
I keep a servant fee'd. I will to-morrow,
And betimes I will, to the weird sisters:
More shall they speak; for now I am bent to know,
By the worst means, the worst. For mine own good,
All causes shall give way: I am in blood
Stepp'd in so far that, should I wade no more,
Returning were as tedious as go o'er:
Strange things I have in head, that will to hand;
Which must be acted ere they may be scann'd.

*I hear it through the grapevine, but I will send
for him. All of them have a servant in their
house who is paid by me. I will go tomorrow,
early in the morning, to talk to the witches.
I will ask them to tell me more, for now I am
determined to know what the worst will be in
the worst way. I have stepped in blood so deep
that even if I were to kill no more, not to do so
would be just as difficult. I have strange
things in my head that I want to make happen.
I must act on them before I think about them
too much.*

LADY MACBETH
You lack the season of all natures, sleep.

You should get some sleep.

MACBETH
Come, we'll to sleep. My strange and self-abuse
Is the initiate fear that wants hard use:
We are yet but young in deed.

*Come, let's get some sleep.
My strange hallucinations are due to my fear.
We are new to committing such crimes.*

Exeunt

Scene V

A Heath

Thunder. Enter the three Witches meeting HECATE

First Witch

Why, how now, Hecate! you look angerly.

How are you, Hecate! You look angry.

HECATE

Have I not reason, beldams as you are,
Saucy and overbold? How did you dare
To trade and traffic with Macbeth
In riddles and affairs of death;
And I, the mistress of your charms,
The close contriver of all harms,
Was never call'd to bear my part,
Or show the glory of our art?
And, which is worse, all you have done
Hath been but for a wayward son,
Spiteful and wrathful, who, as others do,
Loves for his own ends, not for you.
But make amends now: get you gone,
And at the pit of Acheron
Meet me i' the morning: thither he
Will come to know his destiny:
Your vessels and your spells provide,
Your charms and every thing beside.
I am for the air; this night I'll spend
Unto a dismal and a fatal end:
Great business must be wrought ere noon:
Upon the corner of the moon
There hangs a vaporous drop profound;
I'll catch it ere it come to ground:
And that distill'd by magic sleights
Shall raise such artificial sprites
As by the strength of their illusion
Shall draw him on to his confusion:
He shall spurn fate, scorn death, and bear
He hopes 'bove wisdom, grace and fear:
And you all know, security
Is mortals' chiefest enemy.

*I have reason to be angry, you old hags!
You were disobedient and bold.
How dare you deal Macbeth
riddles and matters about death.
And you never consulted me, the mistress of
your charms and
contriver of all harms. You never
even asked my advice. And, even
worse, all you have done
was for a man who is full of spite
and anger and greed. But you can make
it better now. Go away now, and meet
me in the morning at the pit in the river
Acheron. Macbeth will come there
to learn his destiny. Bring your vessels
and your spells and
your charms and
everything else.
I'm going to fly. I'll spend the night figuring
out a dismal and fatal end. Many things need
to be done before noon.
On the corner of the moon hangs
a profound drop of vapor. I will catch it
before it can hit the ground and distill it
with magic deceptions. It will raise such
unreal ghosts that the mere power of their
illusion will draw Macbeth on toward
confusion.
He will scorn fate and death and
believe he is above wisdom, grace and fear.
And, as you know, too much confidence
is the enemy of man.*

Music and a song within: 'Come away, come away,' & c

Hark! I am call'd; my little spirit, see,

Listen! I am being called. I see my little spirit

Sits in a foggy cloud, and stays for me.   *sitting in a foggy cloud, waiting for me.*

Exit

First Witch
Come, let's make haste; she'll soon be back again.   *C'mon, let's hurry. She'll be back again soon.*

Exeunt

Scene VI

Forres. The Palace.

Enter LENNOX and another Lord

LENNOX
My former speeches have but hit your thoughts,
Which can interpret further: only, I say,
Things have been strangely borne. The gracious Duncan
Was pitied of Macbeth: marry, he was dead:
And the right-valiant Banquo walk'd too late;
Whom, you may say, if't please you, Fleance kill'd,
For Fleance fled: men must not walk too late.
Who cannot want the thought how monstrous
It was for Malcolm and for Donalbain
To kill their gracious father? damned fact!
How it did grieve Macbeth! did he not straight
In pious rage the two delinquents tear,
That were the slaves of drink and thralls of sleep?
Was not that nobly done? Ay, and wisely too;
For 'twould have anger'd any heart alive
To hear the men deny't. So that, I say,
He has borne all things well: and I do think
That had he Duncan's sons under his key--
As, an't please heaven, he shall not—they should find
What 'twere to kill a father; so should Fleance.
But, peace! for from broad words and 'cause he fail'd
His presence at the tyrant's feast, I hear
Macduff lives in disgrace: sir, can you tell
Where he bestows himself?

Lord
The son of Duncan,
From whom this tyrant holds the due of birth
Lives in the English court, and is received
Of the most pious Edward with such grace
That the malevolence of fortune nothing
Takes from his high respect: thither Macduff
Is gone to pray the holy king, upon his aid
To wake Northumberland and warlike Siward:
That, by the help of these--with Him above
To ratify the work--we may again

The things I've said have been similar to what you've been thinking, and you can figure out what it means. I'm just saying things have played out strangely. The gracious Duncan was pitied by Macbeth, but—keep in mind—it was after he was dead. The highly noble Banquo was out walking too late. If you'd like, you could say Fleance killed him, since Fleance fled: men must not walk too late! Who cannot wonder at how shockingly wrong it was for Malcolm and Donalbain to kill their gracious father? Such a damned act! It caused Macbeth so much grief! So much that he had to fly into an exaggerated rage and kill the drunken and sleepy guards. Wasn't that good of him? Yes, and wise of him, too. It would have angered anyone to hear the men deny it. It looks like he has handled things well. I think that if he had Duncan's sons locked up— and it's a good thing he does not—they would find out what was the punishment for killing a father, and so would Fleance. But, enough about that! I hear Macduff lives in disgrace because he speaks his mind and failed to show up at Macbeth's dinner. Sir, can you tell me where he is keeping himself?

The son of Duncan, Malcolm, whom Macbeth deprived of his birthright, lives in the English court. He has been welcomed by the good Edward with so much grace that he receives much respect despite his bad luck. Macduff went there to ask for Edward's help to join with Northumberland and their lord, Siward, to fight Macbeth, with the help of God above. He wants to put food on our tables, restore sleep to our nights, allow us to have dinners

Give to our tables meat, sleep to our nights,
Free from our feasts and banquets bloody knives,
Do faithful homage and receive free honours:
All which we pine for now: and this report
Hath so exasperate the king that he
Prepares for some attempt of war.

LENNOX
Sent he to Macduff?

Lord
He did: and with an absolute 'Sir, not I,'
The cloudy messenger turns me his back,
And hums, as who should say 'You'll rue the time
That clogs me with this answer.'

LENNOX
And that well might
Advise him to a caution, to hold what distance
His wisdom can provide. Some holy angel
Fly to the court of England and unfold
His message ere he come, that a swift blessing
May soon return to this our suffering country
Under a hand accursed!

Lord
I'll send my prayers with him.

Exeunt

*and celebrations with no bloody, murderous
knives present, and to pay homage to the king
and receive honors freely. Basically, to give
us all that we long for now. This news has
so upset Macbeth that he is
preparing for war.*

Did he send for Macduff?

*He did. And after Macduff said an absolute
'Sir, I will not,' the gloomy messenger turned
his back to me and hummed, as if to say
'You'll regret the time you gave me this
answer.'*

*And that might
cause him to be cautious, and to keep a wise
distance. A holy angel should fly
to the court of England and deliver a message
telling Macduff to return to Scotland and free
this suffering country from the hand of
Macbeth.*

I'll send my prayers with him.

Act IV

Scene I

A Cavern. In the Middle, a Boiling Cauldron.

Thunder. Enter the three Witches

First Witch
Thrice the brinded cat hath mew'd.

The brindled cat has meowed three times.

Second Witch
Thrice and once the hedge-pig whined.

Yes, three times, and once a hedge-hog whined.

Third Witch
Harpier cries 'Tis time, 'tis time.

My spirit companion Harpier cries that it is time.

First Witch
Round about the cauldron go;
In the poison'd entrails throw.
Toad, that under cold stone
Days and nights has thirty-one
Swelter'd venom sleeping got,
Boil thou first i' the charmed pot.

*Round about the cauldron we go,
and into the poison we throw entrails.
A toad that has spent thirty-one
days under a stone sweating
a poisonous sleeping potion
will go into the pot first.*

ALL
Double, double toil and trouble;
Fire burn, and cauldron bubble.

*Double, double the work and trouble;
The fire wall burn, and the cauldron will bubble.*

Second Witch
Fillet of a fenny snake,
In the cauldron boil and bake;
Eye of newt and toe of frog,
Wool of bat and tongue of dog,
Adder's fork and blind-worm's sting,
Lizard's leg and owlet's wing,
For a charm of powerful trouble,
Like a hell-broth boil and bubble.

*A slice of a snake that inhabits the ferns,
goes into the cauldron to boil and bake;
Eye of a salamander and toe of a frog;
Fur of the bat and tongue of a dog;
The forked tongue of a poisonous snake
and the sting of a blind worm;
A lizard's leg and the wing of a baby owl;
This will make a charm of powerful trouble,
boil and bubble like the broth of hell.*

ALL
Double, double toil and trouble;
Fire burn and cauldron bubble.

*Double, double the work and trouble;
The fire will burn, and the cauldron will bubble.*

Third Witch
Scale of dragon, tooth of wolf,
Witches' mummy, maw and gulf
Of the ravin'd salt-sea shark,
Root of hemlock digg'd i' the dark,

*Scale of a dragon and tooth of a wolf;
A witches' mummified skin; the stomach and
throat the stomach and throat of a hungry
shark; Root of hemlock dug up in the dark;*

Liver of blaspheming Jew,
Gall of goat, and slips of yew
Silver'd in the moon's eclipse,
Nose of Turk and Tartar's lips,
Finger of birth-strangled babe
Ditch-deliver'd by a drab,
Make the gruel thick and slab:
Add thereto a tiger's chaudron,
For the ingredients of our cauldron.

liver of an evil-speaking Jew;
Gallbladder of goat and twigs
of yew broken during an eclipse
of the moon; nose of a Turk
and a Tartar's lips; finger
of a baby strangled in birth while delivered in
a ditch by a slovenly woman. Make the potion
thick and pourable. Add a tiger's intestines
to complete the cauldron's ingredients.

ALL
Double, double toil and trouble;
Fire burn and cauldron bubble.

Double, double the work and trouble;
The fire will burn, and the cauldron will
bubble.

Second Witch
Cool it with a baboon's blood,
Then the charm is firm and good.

Cool it off with baboon's blood,
then the charm will be firm and good.

Enter HECATE to the other three Witches

HECATE
O well done! I commend your pains;
And every one shall share i' the gains;
And now about the cauldron sing,
Live elves and fairies in a ring,
Enchanting all that you put in.

You've done well! I applaud your efforts.
And now everyone should share in the profits.
Gather around the cauldron and sing
like elves and fairies in a ring,
enchanting all that you put into it.

Music and a song: 'Black spirits,' & c

HECATE retires

Second Witch
By the pricking of my thumbs,
Something wicked this way comes.
Open, locks,
Whoever knocks!

I can tell by the way my thumbs tingle
that something wicked is coming this way.
Locks, open to
to whoever knocks!

Enter MACBETH

MACBETH
How now, you secret, black, and midnight hags!
What is't you do?

Well, now, you secret, black, and midnight
hags! What are you doing?

ALL
A deed without a name.

We're doing something that has no name.

MACBETH
I conjure you, by that which you profess,
Howe'er you come to know it, answer me:
Though you untie the winds and let them fight
Against the churches; though the yesty waves
Confound and swallow navigation up;
Though bladed corn be lodged and trees
blown down;
Though castles topple on their warders' heads;
Though palaces and pyramids do slope
Their heads to their foundations;
though the treasure
Of nature's germens tumble all together,
Even till destruction sicken; answer me
To what I ask you.

I ask of you, by what you claim to know and
however you know it, to answer me. Even if
you have to let loose winds that will destroy
churches, and send high waves to wash over
ships and swallow them up; if you have to
unearth planted corn and
blow trees down;
even if castles fall on their lodger's heads and
palaces and pyramids crumble into their
foundations; even if you have to mix the
treasures of nature all up together—
even if destruction takes over everything:
answer me
what I ask of you.

First Witch
Speak.

Speak.

Second Witch
Demand.

Demand.

Third Witch
We'll answer.

We'll answer.

First Witch
Say, if thou'dst rather hear it from our mouths,
Or from our masters?

Would you rather hear it from our mouths
or from our master's mouth?

MACBETH
Call 'em; let me see 'em.

Call them. Let me see them.

First Witch
Pour in sow's blood, that hath eaten
Her nine farrow; grease that's sweaten
From the murderer's gibbet throw
Into the flame.

Pour in the blood of a pig that has eaten
her nine piglets and add fat that has
dripped from a murderer's gallows
into the fire.

ALL
Come, high or low;
Thyself and office deftly show!

Come, high and low spirits.
Reveal yourself and show who you are.

Thunder. First Apparition: an armed Head

MACBETH
Tell me, thou unknown power,--

Tell me, you unknown power—

First Witch
He knows thy thought:
Hear his speech, but say thou nought.

He can read your thoughts.
Listen to him, but don't say anything.

First Apparition
Macbeth! Macbeth! Macbeth! beware Macduff;

Beware the thane of Fife. Dismiss me. Enough.

Macbeth! Macbeth! Macbeth! Beware Macduff.
Beware the thane of Fife. Let me go now. Enough.

Descends

MACBETH
Whate'er thou art, for thy good caution, thanks;
Thou hast harp'd my fear aright: but one word more,--

Wherever you have gone—thanks for the warning. You've addressed what I feared, but let me ask you one more thing—

First Witch
He will not be commanded: here's another,
More potent than the first.

He will not be called back. Here's another stronger than the first.

Thunder. Second Apparition: A bloody Child

Second Apparition
Macbeth! Macbeth! Macbeth!

Macbeth! Macbeth! Macbeth!

MACBETH
Had I three ears, I'ld hear thee.

If I had three ears, I'd listen with all three.

Second Apparition
Be bloody, bold, and resolute; laugh to scorn
The power of man, for none of woman born
Shall harm Macbeth.

Be bloody, bold and determined. Laugh in scorn at the power of any man, for no man born of a woman shall harm Macbeth.

Descends

MACBETH
Then live, Macduff: what need I fear of thee?
But yet I'll make assurance double sure,
And take a bond of fate: thou shalt not live;
That I may tell pale-hearted fear it lies,
And sleep in spite of thunder.

Then Macduff may as well live.
Why should I be afraid of him?
But, just to be double sure and to seal my fate, I will have him killed. That way I can tell my fear it lies and sleep at night in spite of everything.

Thunder. Third Apparition: a Child crowned, with a tree in his hand

What is this

What is this

That rises like the issue of a king,
And wears upon his baby-brow the round
And top of sovereignty?

ALL
Listen, but speak not to't.

Third Apparition
Be lion-mettled, proud; and take no care
Who chafes, who frets, or where conspirers are:
Macbeth shall never vanquish'd be until
Great Birnam wood to high Dunsinane hill
Shall come against him.

Descends

MACBETH
That will never be
Who can impress the forest, bid the tree
Unfix his earth-bound root?
Sweet bodements! good!
Rebellion's head, rise never till the wood
Of Birnam rise, and our high-placed Macbeth
Shall live the lease of nature, pay his breath
To time and mortal custom. Yet my heart
Throbs to know one thing: tell me, if your art
Can tell so much: shall Banquo's issue ever
Reign in this kingdom?

ALL
Seek to know no more.

MACBETH
I will be satisfied: deny me this,
And an eternal curse fall on you! Let me know.
Why sinks that cauldron? and what noise is this?

Hautboys

First Witch
Show!

Second Witch
Show!

Third Witch

---

*that rises like the son of a king
and wears a crown on top of its baby head?*

Listen, but don't speak to it.

*Be courageous like a lion, and proud, and
don't care about who is annoyed by you, or
who plans and plots against you. Macbeth will
not be beat until great Birnam Wood marches
to fight at high Dunsinane Hill.*

*That will never happen.
Who can order the forest
and command the tree to pull its roots from
the ground?
These are good things to hear! I can not be
overtaken until the woods of Birnam walk, and
I shall be king all of my natural life. Yet my
heart pounds to know one more thing. Tell me,
if you can see so much: will Banquo's sons
ever reign
in this kingdom?*

Do not ask any more questions.

*No, I must know! If you don't tell me, an
eternal curse will fall on you! Tell me now.
Why is the cauldron sinking? What is that
noise?*

Show!

Show!

Show!

Show!

ALL
Show his eyes, and grieve his heart;
Come like shadows, so depart!

Show him, and make him grieve.
Come like shadows, and depart the same way!

A show of Eight Kings, the last with a glass in his hand; GHOST OF BANQUO following

MACBETH
Thou art too like the spirit of Banquo: down!
Thy crown does sear mine eye-balls. And thy hair,
Thou other gold-bound brow, is like the first.
A third is like the former. Filthy hags!
Why do you show me this? A fourth! Start, eyes!
What, will the line stretch out to the crack
of doom?
Another yet! A seventh! I'll see no more:
And yet the eighth appears, who bears a glass
Which shows me many more; and some I see
That two-fold balls and treble scepters carry:
Horrible sight! Now, I see, 'tis true;
For the blood-bolter'd Banquo smiles upon me,
And points at them for his.

You look too much like the ghost of Banquo!
Go away! Your crown makes my eyes hurt.
And your blond hair is like the hair of the
first. The third looks just like the second.
Filthy hags! Why do you show me this? A
fourth! My eyes are bulging! Will this line
stretch out all the way to the end
of time? And another! A seventh! I don't want
to see anymore. And yet the eighth appears
who carries a mirror that shows me many
more. Some have two parted balls and three
scepters! This is a horrible sight! Now I see
that it's true. Banquo, with his hair clotted
with blood, smiles at me, and points at them
as his sons.

Apparitions vanish

What, is this so?

Is it true?

First Witch
Ay, sir, all this is so: but why
Stands Macbeth thus amazedly?
Come, sisters, cheer we up his sprites,
And show the best of our delights:
I'll charm the air to give a sound,
While you perform your antic round:
That this great king may kindly say,
Our duties did his welcome pay.

Yes, sir, it is all true. But why
are you so confused? Come, sisters,
let's cheer him up and show him
the best of our magic. I'll charm the air
to make music while you dance,
while you dance, so that
the great king may kindly say we did
our duty to entertain him.

Music. The witches dance and then vanish, with HECATE

MACBETH
Where are they? Gone? Let this pernicious hour
Stand aye accursed in the calendar!
Come in, without there!

Where are they? Gone? Let this evil hour
be marked as cursed in the calendar.
Whoever is out there, come in!

Enter LENNOX

LENNOX
What's your grace's will?

What would you like?

MACBETH
Saw you the weird sisters?

Did you see the witches?

LENNOX
No, my lord.

No, my lord.

MACBETH
Came they not by you?

They didn't pass you?

LENNOX
No, indeed, my lord.

Definitely not, my lord.

MACBETH
Infected be the air whereon they ride;
And damn'd all those that trust them! I did hear
The galloping of horse: who was't came by?

*The air they ride on is infected, and all who
trust them are damned. I heard the galloping
of horses. Who came by?*

LENNOX
'Tis two or three, my lord, that bring you word
Macduff is fled to England.

*Two or three men, my lord, who are here
to let you know Macduff has fled to England.*

MACBETH
Fled to England!

Fled to England!

LENNOX
Ay, my good lord.

Yes, my good lord.

MACBETH
Time, thou anticipatest my dread exploits:
The flighty purpose never is o'ertook
Unless the deed go with it; from this moment
The very firstlings of my heart shall be
The firstlings of my hand. And even now,
To crown my thoughts with acts,
be it thought and done:
The castle of Macduff I will surprise;
Seize upon Fife; give to the edge o' the sword
His wife, his babes, and all unfortunate souls
That trace him in his line. No boasting like a fool;
This deed I'll do before this purpose cool.
But no more sights!--Where are these gentlemen?

*Time, you have guessed my terrible plans.
The intent to act is often overtaken by time.
From this moment on,
I will act immediately
on every impulse in my heart.
I will start now to put my thoughts
into action, and will
surprise Macduff's castle with an attack.
I will seize all of Fife, and have his wife, his
babies, and all those unfortunate enough to be
related to him killed. I will not boast about
doing this; I will simply do it before my
intention cools. But no more visions!—*

Come, bring me where they are.

Exeunt

Scene II

Fife. Macduff's Castle.

Enter LADY MACDUFF, her Son, and ROSS

LADY MACDUFF
What had he done, to make him fly the land?

What did he do, to make him flee the country?

ROSS
You must have patience, madam.

You must have patience, madam.

LADY MACDUFF
He had none:
His flight was madness: when our actions do not,
Our fears do make us traitors.

He had no patience. His flight was crazy.
Even if we aren't traitors, we are going to
look like traitors if we run away.

ROSS
You know not
Whether it was his wisdom or his fear.

You don't know
whether he did it out of wisdom or fear.

LADY MACDUFF
Wisdom! to leave his wife, to leave his babes,
His mansion and his titles in a place
From whence himself does fly? He loves us not;
He wants the natural touch: for the poor wren,
The most diminutive of birds, will fight,
Her young ones in her nest, against the owl.
All is the fear and nothing is the love;
As little is the wisdom, where the flight
So runs against all reason.

Wisdom! To leave his wife and his babies,
his home and his titles in a place he himself
runs away from? He doesn't love us.
He lacks the natural instinct to protect.
Even the skinny little wren—the smallest
of birds—will fight to protect her nest
against the owl. He is full of fear
and is showing no love. There's nothing wise
about such an unreasonable flight.

ROSS
My dearest coz,
I pray you, school yourself: but for your husband,
He is noble, wise, judicious, and best knows
The fits o' the season. I dare not speak
much further;
But cruel are the times, when we are traitors
And do not know ourselves, when we hold rumour
From what we fear, yet know not what we fear,
But float upon a wild and violent sea
Each way and move. I take my leave of you:
Shall not be long but I'll be here again:
Things at the worst will cease, or else climb upward
To what they were before. My pretty cousin,

My dearest cousin, I beg you, have patience.
As far as your husband goes, he in noble,
wise, judicious and knows the ways of the
times. I shouldn't say much more. But these
are cruel times when we are called traitors
and do not know why. We hear rumors that
make us afraid, but we do not know what we
fear. We float on a wild and violent sea and
move back and forth. I must leave, but it
won't be long before I come back. Things at
their worse will either stop or return to what
they were before. My pretty cousin,

Blessing upon you!

I give you my blessing.

LADY MACDUFF
Father'd he is, and yet he's fatherless.

He is a father and yet he is fatherless.

ROSS
I am so much a fool, should I stay longer,
It would be my disgrace and your discomfort:
I take my leave at once.

*I am feeling so foolish. If I stay longer
I might disgrace myself and make you feel
uncomfortable. I will leave at once.*

Exit

LADY MACDUFF
Sirrah, your father's dead;
And what will you do now? How will you live?

*Sir, your father's dead.
What will you do now? How will you live?*

Son
As birds do, mother.

As birds do, mother.

LADY MACDUFF
What, with worms and flies?

*What do you mean, that you'll eat worms and
flies?*

Son
With what I get, I mean; and so do they.

*I mean by what I find. They get by on what
they find.*

LADY MACDUFF
Poor bird! thou'ldst never fear the net nor lime,
The pitfall nor the gin.

*Pathetic bird! You don't know enough to fear
the nets and glue boards and other traps.*

Son
Why should I, mother?
Poor birds they are not set for.
My father is not dead, for all your saying.

*Why should I know that stuff, mother?
No one hunts for pathetic birds.
My father is not dead, even though you say he
is.*

LADY MACDUFF
Yes, he is dead; how wilt thou do for a father?

*Yes, he is dead. What will you do without a
father?*

Son
Nay, how will you do for a husband?

*No, the question is—what will you do without
a husband?*

LADY MACDUFF
Why, I can buy me twenty at any market.

I can buy twenty of them at any market.

Son
Then you'll buy 'em to sell again.

Then you'll buy them to sell again.

LADY MACDUFF
Thou speak'st with all thy wit: and yet, i' faith,
With wit enough for thee.

*You speak with all of your intelligence, which,
to be fair, is enough intelligence for you.*

Son
Was my father a traitor, mother?

Was my father a traitor, mother?

LADY MACDUFF
Ay, that he was.

Yes, he was.

Son
What is a traitor?

What is a traitor?

LADY MACDUFF
Why, one that swears and lies.

It's one who swears to do something but lies.

Son
And be all traitors that do so?

And do all traitors do that?

LADY MACDUFF
Every one that does so is a traitor,
and must be hanged.

*Everyone who does that is a traitor,
and must be hanged.*

Son
And must they all be hanged that swear and lie?

*Everyone who swears and lies must be
hanged?*

LADY MACDUFF
Every one.

Every one.

Son
Who must hang them?

Who hangs them?

LADY MACDUFF
Why, the honest men.

The honest men do.

Son
Then the liars and swearers are fools,
for there are liars and swearers enow to beat
the honest men and hang up them.

*Then the liars and swearers are fools,
because there are enough liars and swearers
to beat the honest men and hang them.*

LADY MACDUFF
Now, God help thee, poor monkey!
But how wilt thou do for a father?

*God help you, my poor monkey!
But what will you do without a father?*

Son
If he were dead, you'ld weep for

If he were dead, you'd be crying for him

him: if you would not, it were a good sign
that I should quickly have a new father.

If you don't cry, it is a good sign that I will soon have a new father.

LADY MACDUFF
Poor prattler, how thou talk'st!

Silly boy, how you talk!

Enter a Messenger

Messenger
Bless you, fair dame! I am not to you known,
Though in your state of honour I am perfect.
I doubt some danger does approach you nearly:
If you will take a homely man's advice,
Be not found here; hence, with your little ones.
To fright you thus, methinks, I am too savage;
To do worse to you were fell cruelty,
Which is too nigh your person.
Heaven preserve you!
I dare abide no longer.

Bless you, lovely lady. You do not know me, but I know who you are and of your state of honor. I know that danger is heading your way. If you want to take a common man's advice— don't allow yourself to be found here with your children. You must think I am awful to frighten you like this, but I think it would be worse if I said nothing and you were cruelly harmed. Harm is nearby. Heaven help you! I can not stay here any longer.

Exit

LADY MACDUFF
Whither should I fly?
I have done no harm. But I remember now
I am in this earthly world; where to do harm
Is often laudable, to do good sometime
Accounted dangerous folly: why then, alas,
Do I put up that womanly defence,
To say I have done no harm?

Where should I go? I've done no wrong. But I remember now I am in this earthly world, where doing harm is often praised, and to do good is seen as silly and dangerous. Why do I even bother to put up a womanly defense by saying I have done no harm?

Enter Murderers

What are these faces?

Who are these people?

First Murderer
Where is your husband?

Where is your husband?

LADY MACDUFF
I hope, in no place so unsanctified
Where such as thou mayst find him.

I hope he's not in an unholy place where people like you can find him.

First Murderer
He's a traitor.

He's a traitor.

Son
Thou liest, thou shag-hair'd villain!   *You lie, you shaggy haired villain!*

First Murderer
What, you egg!   *What! You egg!*

Stabbing him

Young fry of treachery!   *You son of treachery!*

Son
He has kill'd me, mother: *He has killed me, mother—*
Run away, I pray you!   *I beg you to run away!*

Dies
Exit LADY MACDUFF, crying 'Murder!' Exeunt Murderers, following her

Scene III

England. Before the King's Palace.

Enter MALCOLM and MACDUFF

MALCOLM
Let us seek out some desolate shade, and there
Weep our sad bosoms empty.

Let's find a dismal shady place and sit down and cry our hearts out.

MACDUFF
Let us rather
Hold fast the mortal sword, and like good men
Bestride our down-fall'n birthdom: each new morn
New widows howl, new orphans cry, new sorrows
Strike heaven on the face, that it resounds
As if it felt with Scotland and yell'd out
Like syllable of dolour.

Let's hold onto our swords, instead, and defend our fallen birthplace like good men. Every new day, new widows howl, new orphans cry, new sorrows slap heaven on the face so loudly that it sounds as if heaven feels Scotland's pain and cries out in grief.

MALCOLM
What I believe I'll wail,
What know believe, and what I can redress,
As I shall find the time to friend, I will.
What you have spoke, it may be so perchance.
This tyrant, whose sole name blisters our tongues,
Was once thought honest: you have loved him well.
He hath not touch'd you yet. I am young;
but something
You may deserve of him through me, and wisdom
To offer up a weak poor innocent lamb
To appease an angry god.

I deplore what I believe is wrong. I believe what I know. I will set right what I can when I find the proper time. What you just said might be true. This tyrant, whose name blisters our tongues, was once considered honest. You were loved by him. He hasn't touched you yet. I am young and don't know much, but maybe you want something from him and you're thinking it might be wise to offer up a poor, innocent lamb like myself to please the angry god-like Macbeth.

MACDUFF
I am not treacherous.

I am not treacherous.

MALCOLM
But Macbeth is.
A good and virtuous nature may recoil
In an imperial charge. But I shall crave
your pardon;
That which you are my thoughts cannot transpose:
Angels are bright still, though the brightest fell;
Though all things foul would wear the brows
of grace,
Yet grace must still look so.

But Macbeth is A good and honest nature might shrink back under a royal order. But I beg your pardon— just because I'm thinking it doesn't make it so. Angels are still bright even though the brightest angel fell. And although everything that is bad would like to appear like grace, Grace must look like grace, too.

MACDUFF
I have lost my hopes.

I have lost my hopes.

MALCOLM
Perchance even there where I did find my doubts.
Why in that rawness left you wife and child,
Those precious motives, those strong knots of love,
Without leave-taking? I pray you,
Let not my jealousies be your dishonours,
But mine own safeties. You may be rightly just,
Whatever I shall think.

Maybe you lost them where I found my doubts.
Why did you leave your wife and children
in that cruel place—those precious reasons
for being, those strong ties of love—without
saying goodbye? But please don't feel shame
because of my suspicions. I'm just trying
to keep myself safe. You may be entirely just
and good, despite what I think.

MACDUFF
Bleed, bleed, poor country!
Great tyranny! lay thou thy basis sure,
For goodness dare not cheque thee: wear thou
thy wrongs;
The title is affeer'd! Fare thee well, lord:
I would not be the villain that thou think'st
For the whole space that's in the tyrant's grasp,
And the rich East to boot.

Bleed, bleed, poor country!
Great tyranny! You've lain a such a solid
foundation that good people will not even
dare to try and control you. Wear your
wrongs easily because your title is not in
danger. Goodbye, lord. I would not be the
villain you think I am for everything in that
tyrant's grasp, with the wealth of the East
thrown in, as well.

MALCOLM
Be not offended:
I speak not as in absolute fear of you.
I think our country sinks beneath the yoke;
It weeps, it bleeds; and each new day a gash
Is added to her wounds: I think withal
There would be hands uplifted in my right;
And here from gracious England have I offer
Of goodly thousands: but, for all this,
of good
When I shall tread upon the tyrant's head,
Or wear it on my sword, yet my poor country
Shall have more vices than it had before,
More suffer and more sundry ways than ever,
By him that shall succeed.

Please don't be offended.
I'm not saying these things because I
completely distrust you. I think our country
sinks under the weight of Macbeth's
oppression. It weeps, it bleeds, and each day a
deep new cut is added to her wounds. I think
many men would volunteer to fight in my
name. England has offered thousands

soldiers. Still, when I place my boot upon
Macbeth's head, or wear it on my sword, my
poor country will still have more troubles than
it had before. There will be more suffering in
more ways than now under he who follows
Macbeth.

MACDUFF
What should he be?

Who would that be?

MALCOLM
It is myself I mean: in whom I know
All the particulars of vice so grafted
That, when they shall be open'd, black Macbeth
Will seem as pure as snow, and the poor state

It is myself I refer to. I know all of the faults
in myself that—once revealed—will make
evil Macbeth seem as pure as snow, and
the poor country will see him as a lamb

Esteem him as a lamb, being compared
With my confineless harms.

compared with what
I am capable of doing.

MACDUFF
Not in the legions
Of horrid hell can come a devil more damn'd
In evils to top Macbeth.

Not in all of hell
can come a devil capable
of outdoing Macbeth.

MALCOLM
I grant him bloody,
Luxurious, avaricious, false, deceitful,
Sudden, malicious, smacking of every sin
That has a name: but there's no bottom, none,
In my voluptuousness: your wives, your daughters,
Your matrons and your maids, could not fill up
The cistern of my lust, and my desire
All continent impediments would o'erbear
That did oppose my will: better Macbeth
Than such an one to reign.

It's true, he is murderous, lecherous, greedy,
lying, deceitful, unpredictable, malicious, and
carries every sin that can be named. But
there's no bottom— none—to my own
lustfulness: your wives, your daughters,
your dignified older women and your young
women could not possible fill the deep well of
my lust. My desire would overcome all
resistance and obstacles, I would so impose
my will. You'd be better off with Macbeth
than with someone like me.

MACDUFF
Boundless intemperance
In nature is a tyranny; it hath been
The untimely emptying of the happy throne
And fall of many kings. But fear not yet
To take upon you what is yours: you may
Convey your pleasures in a spacious plenty,
And yet seem cold, the time you may so hoodwink.
We have willing dames enough: there cannot be
That vulture in you, to devour so many
As will to greatness dedicate themselves,
Finding it so inclined.

Boundless lack of control of lustful desires
is a sort of tyranny. It has resulted in the
premature emptying of the throne and the fall
of many kings. But don't fear taking the crown
that is yours. You many find your pleasure
everywhere and still appear cold. No one
needs to know. You can deceive them. We
have many willing women—you couldn't
possibly devour so many as will give
themselves to the king, once they know he
desires them.

MALCOLM
With this there grows
In my most ill-composed affection such
A stanchless avarice that, were I king,
I should cut off the nobles for their lands,
Desire his jewels and this other's house:
And my more-having would be as a sauce
To make me hunger more; that I should forge
Quarrels unjust against the good and loyal,
Destroying them for wealth.

Along with being incredibly lustful, I am
also extremely greedy.
If I were the king,
I should take away nobleman's land.
I would desire his jewels and another's house.
The more I got, the more I would want.
I would create arguments between good
and loyal men so they would be destroyed
and I would gain their wealth.

MACDUFF
This avarice

This greed

Sticks deeper, grows with more pernicious root
Than summer-seeming lust, and it hath been
The sword of our slain kings: yet do not fear;
Scotland hath foisons to fill up your will.
Of your mere own: all these are portable,
With other graces weigh'd.

MALCOLM
But I have none: the king-becoming graces,
As justice, verity, temperance, stableness,
Bounty, perseverance, mercy, lowliness,
Devotion, patience, courage, fortitude,
I have no relish of them, but abound
In the division of each several crime,
Acting it many ways. Nay, had I power, I should
Pour the sweet milk of concord into hell,
Uproar the universal peace, confound
All unity on earth.

MACDUFF
O Scotland, Scotland!

MALCOLM
If such a one be fit to govern, speak:
I am as I have spoken.

MACDUFF
Fit to govern!
No, not to live. O nation miserable,
With an untitled tyrant bloody-scepter'd,
When shalt thou see thy wholesome days again,
Since that the truest issue of thy throne
By his own interdiction stands accursed,
And does blaspheme his breed? Thy royal father
Was a most sainted king: the queen that bore thee,
Oftener upon her knees than on her feet,
Died every day she lived. Fare thee well!
These evils thou repeat'st upon thyself
Have banish'd me from Scotland. O my breast,
Thy hope ends here!

MALCOLM
Macduff, this noble passion,
Child of integrity, hath from my soul
Wiped the black scruples, reconciled my thoughts
To thy good truth and honour. Devilish Macbeth

*you speak of goes deeper
than the lust, and it will remain longer,
unlike lust. It has been the end to many kings.
Still, don't worry. Scotland has a great
number of riches to satisfy you. These things
can easily be dealt with, and your strengths
outweigh them.*

*But I don't have any of the graces kings
require, like justice, truth, self-restraint,
stableness, generosity, mercy, humbleness,
devotion, patience, courage, strength—I have
none of them, but I have plenty of each
of the vices which act out in every way.
Don't doubt it: if I had the power, I would
throw harmony to hell, upset the universal
peace, and defeat
all unity on earth.*

Oh, Scotland! Scotland!

*If you think such a person as me is fit
to rule, then say so. I am what I say I am.*

*Fit to govern!
You are not even fit to live! Oh, miserable
nation with an untitled bloody-handed tyrant
on the throne, when will you see wholesome
days again, since the true birthright of the
throne, by his own admission, is cursed and a
disgrace to his own family. Your royal father,
Duncan, was worthy of being a saint. Your
mother, the queen, was on her knees in prayer
more often than on her feet, she felt so
indifferent to worldly things. Good-bye!
These evils you say you have in yourself have
driven me out of Scotland. Oh, my heart. The
hope ends here!*

*Macduff, this noble outburst on your part
reveals your integrity. It's wiped away the
dark doubts that were in my soul, and has
restored thoughts of you as truthful and*

By many of these trains hath sought to win me
Into his power, and modest wisdom plucks me
From over-credulous haste: but God above
Deal between thee and me! for even now
I put myself to thy direction, and
Unspeak mine own detraction, here abjure
The taints and blames I laid upon myself,
For strangers to my nature. I am yet
Unknown to woman, never was forsworn,
Scarcely have coveted what was mine own,
At no time broke my faith, would not betray
The devil to his fellow and delight
No less in truth than life: my first false speaking
Was this upon myself: what I am truly,
Is thine and my poor country's to command:
Whither indeed, before thy here-approach,
Old Siward, with ten thousand warlike men,
Already at a point, was setting forth.
Now we'll together; and the chance of goodness
Be like our warranted quarrel! Why are you silent?

of you as truthful and honest. The devil, Macbeth, has often tried to win me to his side with skills of deception. Because of that, I try to be wise and not believe too quickly. But with God's blessing, I would join with you. I take back all the things I just told you about me. The faults I listed are not in me. I am still a virgin, I've never lied. I hardly care about the things I own, let alone the possessions of others. I've never gone back on my word, would not betray the devil himself, and take as much pleasure in truth as I do in life. Telling you the things I told you was my first lie. Who I truly am is ready to be at your poor country's command. Indeed, before you came here, old Siward and ten thousand soldiers were already gathered and setting forth. Now we can fight together, and may the chance of success equal that of our justified dispute. Why are you not saying anything?

MACDUFF
Such welcome and unwelcome things at once
'Tis hard to reconcile.

Such welcome and unwelcome things at once is hard to come to terms with.

Enter a Doctor

MALCOLM
Well; more anon.—
Comes the king forth, I pray you?

We'll speak more soon.
Is King Edward coming out?

Doctor
Ay, sir; there are a crew of wretched souls
That stay his cure: their malady convinces
The great assay of art; but at his touch—
Such sanctity hath heaven given his hand--
They presently amend.

Yes, sir. There are a lot of sick people in need of his cure. Their illness puzzles modern medicine, but when he lays his hands on them, the power invested in him by heaven cures them.

MALCOLM
I thank you, doctor.

Thank you, doctor.

Exit Doctor

MACDUFF
What's the disease he means?

What disease does he mean?

MALCOLM
'Tis call'd the evil:
A most miraculous work in this good king;
Which often, since my here-remain in England,
I have seen him do. How he solicits heaven,
Himself best knows: but strangely-visited people,
All swoln and ulcerous, pitiful to the eye,
The mere despair of surgery, he cures,
Hanging a golden stamp about their necks,
Put on with holy prayers: and 'tis spoken,
To the succeeding royalty he leaves
The healing benediction. With this strange virtue,
He hath a heavenly gift of prophecy,
And sundry blessings hang about his throne,
That speak him full of grace.

It's called 'the evil.'
I've seen him do miraculous acts since I've
been in England. How he obtains help from
heaven, only he knows. But people with all
sorts of symptoms— swollen and full of ulcers,
pitiful to look at, beyond the help of surgery—
he cures. He hangs a golden stamp around
their neck and says holy prayers. It's said that
this ability to heal will be passed along the
royal lineage.
Along with this, he has the gift of being able
to see the future, and other sorts of gifts, as
well. He seems a king graced by God.

Enter ROSS

MACDUFF
See, who comes here?

Who is that coming here?

MALCOLM
My countryman; but yet I know him not.

He's from Scotland, but I don't know him yet.

MACDUFF
My ever-gentle cousin, welcome hither.

My gentle cousin, welcome here.

MALCOLM
I know him now. Good God, betimes remove
The means that makes us strangers!

I recognize him now. Good God, it's time
to remove the interventions that make us
strangers!

ROSS
Sir, amen.

So be it, sir.

MACDUFF
Stands Scotland where it did?

Is Scotland still as it was?

ROSS
Alas, poor country!
Almost afraid to know itself. It cannot
Be call'd our mother, but our grave; where nothing,
But who knows nothing, is once seen to smile;
Where sighs and groans and shrieks that
rend the air
Are made, not mark'd; where violent sorrow seems
A modern ecstasy; the dead man's knell

Poor country!
It's almost afraid to know itself.
It cannot be called our mother any longer; it
is our grave. Where nobody smiles except
those who know nothing. Where sighs and
groans and shrieks are made with no notice.
Where violent sorrow seems like ectasy.
When the bells ring for the funeral, people

Is there scarce ask'd for who; and good men's lives
Expire before the flowers in their caps,
Dying or ere they sicken.

rarely ask who it is. Good men die before the flowers in their caps wilt. They die before they sicken.

MACDUFF
O, relation
Too nice, and yet too true!

Oh, my relative.
Your report is nicely delivered, and too true.

MALCOLM
What's the newest grief?

What's the latest news?

ROSS
That of an hour's age doth hiss the speaker:
Each minute teems a new one.

News an hour old disproves the speaker.
Every minute brings new news.

MACDUFF
How does my wife?

How is my wife?

ROSS
Why, well.

She is well.

MACDUFF
And all my children?

And all of my children?

ROSS
Well too.

They are also well.

MACDUFF
The tyrant has not batter'd at their peace?

The tyrant has not disturbed their peace?

ROSS
No; they were well at peace when I did leave 'em.

No, they were well and at peace when I left them.

MACDUFF
But not a niggard of your speech: how goes't?

Don't be stingy with your speech. How are things?

ROSS
When I came hither to transport the tidings,
Which I have heavily borne, there ran a rumor
Of many worthy fellows that were out;
Which was to my belief witness'd the rather,
For that I saw the tyrant's power a-foot:
Now is the time of help; your eye in Scotland
Would create soldiers, make our women fight,
To doff their dire distresses.

When I came here to deliver my news, which I have carried sadly, there was a rumor that many good fellows were turning against Macbeth. I saw Macbeth's troops moving. Now is the time we need help. Your presence in Scotland would cause men to become soldiers, and even women would fight to end the current distress.

MALCOLM
Be't their comfort
We are coming thither: gracious England hath
Lent us good Siward and ten thousand men;
An older and a better soldier none
That Christendom gives out.

They will be comforted. I am coming to Scotland. The gracious king of England has lent us good Siward and ten thousand men. An older and better solider than Siward does not exist in the Christian world.

ROSS
Would I could answer
This comfort with the like! But I have words
That would be howl'd out in the desert air,
Where hearing should not latch them.

I wish I could answer with news that would comfort in the same way. But I have words that should only be howled in the desert air where nobody can hear them.

MACDUFF
What concern they?
The general cause? or is it a fee-grief
Due to some single breast?

Who do they concern? Is it for the general cause? Or will the grief affect one person alone?

ROSS
No mind that's honest
But in it shares some woe; though the main part
Pertains to you alone.

No mind that's honest will be able to not share in the grief. But it mostly concerns you alone.

MACDUFF
If it be mine,
Keep it not from me, quickly let me have it.

If it is mine, don't keep it from me. Tell it to me quickly.

ROSS
Let not your ears despise my tongue for ever,
Which shall possess them with the heaviest sound
That ever yet they heard.

Don't let your ears hate my tongue forever, when they hear the most sorrowful thing they have ever heard.

MACDUFF
Hum! I guess at it

Hmm. I think I can guess what you are going to say.

ROSS
Your castle is surprised; your wife and babes
Savagely slaughter'd: to relate the manner,
Were, on the quarry of these murder'd deer,
To add the death of you.

Your castle was attacked. Your wife and children are dead. To tell you how it was done would only add to the death of you.

MALCOLM
Merciful heaven!
What, man! ne'er pull your hat upon your brows;
Give sorrow words: the grief that does not speak

Merciful heaven! Listen, man! Don't keep your grief inside. Speak your sorrow. Grief that is not expressed

Whispers the o'er-fraught heart and bids it break. | *will whisper in your heart until it breaks.*

MACDUFF
My children too? | *They killed my children, too?*

ROSS
Wife, children, servants, all
That could be found. | *They killed your wife, your children, your servants— they killed everyone that could be found.*

MACDUFF
And I must be from thence!
My wife kill'd too? | *And I had to be away from there! They killed my wife, too?*

ROSS
I have said. | *I said they did.*

MALCOLM
Be comforted:
Let's make us medicines of our great revenge,
To cure this deadly grief. | *Let us find comfort in revenge to cure this awful grief.*

MACDUFF
He has no children. All my pretty ones?
Did you say all? O hell-kite! All?
What, all my pretty chickens and their dam
At one fell swoop? | *Macbeth has no children. All of my pretty ones? Did you say all of them? Oh, hellish bird! All? All of my pretty children and their mother in one fell swoop?*

MALCOLM
Dispute it like a man. | *Challenge it like a man.*

MACDUFF
I shall do so;
But I must also feel it as a man:
I cannot but remember such things were,
That were most precious to me.
Did heaven look on,
And would not take their part? Sinful Macduff,
They were all struck for thee! naught that I am,
Not for their own demerits, but for mine,
Fell slaughter on their souls. Heaven rest them now! | *I will do so. But I also must feel it like a man. I cannot help but remember those who were so precious to me. Did heaven look on, and not take their side? I am full of sin. They were all killed because of me! Not for their own sins, but for mine they were killed. May they rest in heaven now!*

MALCOLM
Be this the whetstone of your sword: let grief
Convert to anger; blunt not the heart, enrage it. | *Let this sharpen your sword. Let grief change to anger. Instead of dulling the heart, let grief inflame it.*

MACDUFF
O, I could play the woman with mine eyes | *Oh, I could cry like a woman and brag of*

And braggart with my tongue! But, gentle heavens,
Cut short all intermission; front to front
Bring thou this fiend of Scotland and myself;
Within my sword's length set him; if he 'scape,
Heaven forgive him too!

MALCOLM
This tune goes manly.
Come, go we to the king; our power is ready;
Our lack is nothing but our leave; Macbeth
Is ripe for shaking, and the powers above
Put on their instruments.
Receive what cheer you may:
The night is long that never finds the day.

Exeunt

*what I will do. But, gentle heavens, let's cut it
short. Bring me face to face with this fiend of
Scotland.*
*Put him within my sword's length. If he
escapes, Heaven forgive him!*

Now you are sounding like a man.
*Come, let's go to the king. Our armies are
ready. We lack nothing at this point but
departure. Macbeth is ripe for picking, and
may the powers above give us aid. Find what
cheer you can.*
It's a long night that never finds the day.

ACT V

Scene I

Dunsinane. Ante-Room in the Castle.

Enter a Doctor of Physic and a Waiting-Gentlewoman

Doctor

I have two nights watched with you,
but can perceive
no truth in your report.
When was it she last walked?

*I have watched with you for two nights,
but can find
no truth in your report.
When did she last sleep walk?*

Gentlewoman

Since his majesty went into the field,
I have seen
her rise from her bed, throw her night-gown upon
her, unlock her closet, take forth paper, fold it,
write upon't, read it, afterwards seal it, and again
return to bed; yet all this while in a most fast sleep.

*Since his majesty went into battle,
I have seen
her rise from bed, throw on her nightgown,
unlock her closet, take out paper, fold it,
write on it, read it, seal it up, and return to
bed again. She did all of this while fast asleep.*

Doctor

A great perturbation in nature, to receive at once
the benefit of sleep, and do the effects of
watching! In this slumbery agitation, besides her
walking and other actual performances,
what, at any time, have you heard her say?

*It's a great disturbance, to seem as if you are
asleep, and do the things you do when awake.
In this state— besides her walking and the
things she does—have your
heard her say anything?*

Gentlewoman

That, sir, which I will not report after her.

Yes, sir, but I will not say what it is.

Doctor

You may to me: and 'tis most meet you should.

*You should say it to me, and it would be
helpful if you did.*

Gentlewoman

Neither to you nor any one; having no witness to
confirm my speech.

*I won't say it to you or anyone else.
I was the only one to witness it.*

Enter LADY MACBETH, with a taper

Lo you, here she comes! This is her very guise;
and, upon my life, fast asleep.
Observe her; stand close.

*Look, here she comes! This is how she is
awake, but—upon my life—she is sound
asleep. Watch her. Stay near.*

Doctor

How came she by that light?

How did she get that candle?

Gentlewoman
Why, it stood by her: she has light by her
continually; 'tis her command.

*It was by her bedside. She has light by her all
the time. She requests it.*

Doctor
You see, her eyes are open.

You see, her eyes are open.

Gentlewoman
Ay, but their sense is shut.

Yes, but they don't see anything.

Doctor
What is it she does now?
Look, how she rubs her hands.

What is she doing now?
Look at how she rubs her hands together.

Gentlewoman
It is an accustomed action with her, to seem thus
washing her hands: I have known her continue in
this a quarter of an hour.

*It's a common action with her. She seems to
be washing her hands. I have witnessed her
doing this for at least fifteen minutes.*

LADY MACBETH
Yet here's a spot.

There's still a spot.

Doctor
Hark! she speaks:
I will set down what comes from
her, to satisfy my remembrance the more strongly.

Listen! She speaks!
I will write down what she says
to help me remember it better.

LADY MACBETH
Out, damned spot! out, I say!--One: two: why,
then, 'tis time to do't.--Hell is murky!--Fie, my
lord, fie! a soldier, and afeard? What need we
fear who knows it,
when none can call our power to
account?--Yet who would have thought
the old man
to have had so much blood in him.

*Out, damned spot! Out, I say!—one, two, why
it is time to do it. –Hell is murky!—Nonsense,
my lord, nonsense! A soldier, and afraid? Why
should we be afraid,
when none can call our power
into account?—Who knew the old man would
Who knew the old man would
have so much blood in him?*

Doctor
Do you mark that?

Did you hear that?

LADY MACBETH
The thane of Fife had a wife: where is she now?--
What, will these hands ne'er be clean?--No more o'
that, my lord, no more o' that: you mar all with
this starting.

*The thane of Fife had a wife: where is she
now?— What, will these hands never be
clean?—No more of that, my lord, no more of
that: you'll ruin everything with acting
startled.*

Doctor
Go to, go to;
you have known what you should not.

Go on, go on—
have known what you should not know.

Gentlewoman
She has spoke what she should not, I am sure of
that: heaven knows what she has known.

She has spoken what she should not, I am sure
of it. Heaven knows what she has known.

LADY MACBETH
Here's the smell of the blood still: all the
perfumes of Arabia will not sweeten this little
hand. Oh, oh, oh!

The smell of the blood is still here. All the
perfumes of Arabis will not sweeten this little
hand. Oh, oh, oh!

Doctor
What a sigh is there! The heart is sorely charged.

What a sigh there is. Her heart is very heavy.

Gentlewoman
I would not have such a heart in my bosom for the
dignity of the whole body.

I would not have such a heart in my chest even
if my whole body was dignity.

Doctor
Well, well, well,--

Well, well, well—

Gentlewoman
Pray God it be, sir.

If only it were so, sir.

Doctor
This disease is beyond my practise:
yet I have known
those which have walked in their sleep who have
died holily in their beds.

This disease is beyond me.
Still, I have known
of those who walk in their sleep who died pure
in their beds.

LADY MACBETH
Wash your hands, put on your nightgown;
look not so pale.--
I tell you yet again, Banquo's buried;
he cannot come out on's grave.

Wash your hands and put on your nightgown.
Don't look so pale—I tell you once again:
Banquo's buried. He
cannot come out of his grave.

Doctor
Even so?

However?

LADY MACBETH
To bed, to bed! there's knocking at the gate:
come, come, come, come, give me your hand.

Go to bed, to bed! There's a knocking at the
gate: come, come, come, come—give me your

What's done cannot be undone.—

Exit

Doctor
Will she go now to bed?

Gentlewoman
Directly.

Doctor
Foul whisperings are abroad: unnatural deeds
Do breed unnatural troubles: infected minds
To their deaf pillows will discharge their secrets:
More needs she the divine than the physician.
God, God forgive us all! Look after her;
Remove from her the means of all annoyance,
And still keep eyes upon her. So, good night:
My mind she has mated, and amazed my sight.
I think, but dare not speak.

Gentlewoman
Good night, good doctor.

Exeunt

hand. What's done cannot be undone.—To bed, to bed, to bed!

Will she go to bed now?

Immediately.

Filthy rumors are going around. Unnatural acts cause unnatural troubles. Worried minds will confess their secrets to unhearing pillows. She needs more help than a doctor can give. God, God forgive us all! Look after her. Remove anything that she could use to harm herself, and keep a watch on her. Good night. Her actions have bred thoughts in my mind and amazed my eyes. I am thinking about what I have witnessed, but dare not speak.

Good night, good doctor.

Scene II

The Country Near Dunsinane.

Drum and colours. Enter MENTEITH, CAITHNESS, ANGUS, LENNOX, and Soldiers

MENTEITH
The English power is near, led on by Malcolm,
His uncle Siward and the good Macduff:
Revenges burn in them; for their dear causes
Would to the bleeding and the grim alarm
Excite the mortified man.

The English army is drawing near, led by Malcolm, his uncle Siward, and the good Macduff. Revenge burns in them. Their causes would incite the bloody and dead to rise and fight.

ANGUS
Near Birnam wood
Shall we well meet them; that way are they coming.

We will meet them near Birnam wood. They are coming that way.

CAITHNESS
Who knows if Donalbain be with his brother?

Is Donalbain with his brother?

LENNOX
For certain, sir, he is not: I have a file
Of all the gentry: there is Siward's son,
And many unrough youths that even now
Protest their first of manhood.

For sure, sir, he is not with him. I have a record of all the gentry: there is Siward's son, and many men who are too young to have their first beards.

MENTEITH
What does the tyrant?

What is Macbeth doing?

CAITHNESS
Great Dunsinane he strongly fortifies:
Some say he's mad; others that lesser hate him
Do call it valiant fury: but, for certain,
He cannot buckle his distemper'd cause
Within the belt of rule.

He is fortifying his castle at Dunsinane. Some say he's insane, while those who don't hate him so much call it determined anger. But, to be sure, he cannot control his rage within his range of rule.

ANGUS
Now does he feel
His secret murders sticking on his hands;
Now minutely revolts upbraid his faith-breach;
Those he commands move only in command,
Nothing in love: now does he feel his title
Hang loose about him, like a giant's robe
Upon a dwarfish thief.

*Now he feels
the blood of his secret murders on his hands. Now small armies punish his breach of faith. Those soldiers he commands respond only by duty, not out of love. He feels his title hanging loose on him, like a giant's robe on a dwarfish thief.*

MENTEITH
Who then shall blame
His pester'd senses to recoil and start,
When all that is within him does condemn
Itself for being there?

Who can blame
his senses for drawing back and starting
again, when all that is within him condemns
him to himself?

CAITHNESS
Well, march we on,
To give obedience where 'tis truly owed:
Meet we the medicine of the sickly weal,
And with him pour we in our country's purge
Each drop of us.

Well, let's march on
and give obedience where it is deserved.
We are going to meet the medicine
that will cure our country of this illness—
Malcolm. We will give every drop of our
blood to him.

LENNOX
Or so much as it needs,
To dew the sovereign flower and drown the weeds.
Make we our march towards Birnam.

However much is required to water the royal
flower and drown the weeds. Let's march
towards Birnam.

Exeunt, marching

Scene III

Dunsinane. A room in the Castle.

Enter MACBETH, Doctor, and Attendants

MACBETH
Bring me no more reports; let them fly all:
Till Birnam wood remove to Dunsinane,
I cannot taint with fear. What's the boy Malcolm?
Was he not born of woman? The spirits that know
All mortal consequences have pronounced me thus:
'Fear not, Macbeth; no man that's born of woman
Shall e'er have power upon thee.' Then fly,
false thanes, And mingle with the English epicures:
The mind I sway by and the heart I bear
Shall never sag with doubt nor shake with fear.

*Bring me no more news—let them go.
Until Birnam wood moves to Dunsinane
I need not have any fear. Who's this boy
Malcolm? Wasn't he born of a woman? The
spirits that can see all thing have told me this:
'Fear not, Macbeth, no man that's born of
woman will ever have power over you.' So
leave, disloyal thanes, and mingle
with the dainty English: my mind will not
sway and my heart will never sag with doubt
or shake with fear.*

Enter a Servant

The devil damn thee black,
thou cream-faced loon!
Where got'st thou that goose look?

*May the devil make you black,
you cream-faced loon!
Why do you look so foolish?*

Servant
There is ten thousand—

There are ten thousand—

MACBETH
Geese, villain!

Geese, evil one!

Servant
Soldiers, sir.

Soldiers, sir.

MACBETH
Go prick thy face, and over-red thy fear,
Thou lily-liver'd boy. What soldiers, patch?
Death of thy soul! those linen cheeks of thine
Are counsellors to fear. What soldiers, whey-face?

*Go prick your face to make it red so your fear
does not show, you lily-livered coward. What
soldiers, you clown? Death to your soul!
That white face of yours will make others
fearful. What soldiers, milk-face?*

Servant
The English force, so please you.

The English army.

MACBETH
Take thy face hence.

Take your face out of here.

Exit Servant

Seyton!--I am sick at heart,
When I behold--Seyton, I say!--This push
Will cheer me ever, or disseat me now.
I have lived long enough: my way of life
Is fall'n into the sear, the yellow leaf;
And that which should accompany old age,
As honour, love, obedience, troops of friends,
I must not look to have; but, in their stead,
Curses, not loud but deep, mouth-honour, breath,
Which the poor heart would fain deny,
and dare not. Seyton!

*Seyton!—I am sick at heart when I see—
Seyton, come here!—this battle will encourage
me forever, or it will de-throne me now. I have
lived long enough. My way of life has
withered like a yellow leaf. That which should
keep me company in my old age— such as
honor, love, obedience, lots of friends—
I cannot expect to have. Instead, I have
curses, people who talk about me under their
breath, and life, which my heart would gladly
deny, but dares not. Seyton!*

Enter SEYTON

SEYTON
What is your gracious pleasure?

What would be your pleasure?

MACBETH
What news more?

Is there any more news?

SEYTON
All is confirm'd, my lord, which was reported.

*All that has been reported, my lord, has been
confirmed.*

MACBETH
I'll fight till from my bones my flesh be hack'd.
Give me my armor.

*I'll fight until my flesh is hacked from my
bones. Give me my armor.*

SEYTON
'Tis not needed yet.

You don't need it yet.

MACBETH
I'll put it on.
Send out more horses; skirr the country round;
Hang those that talk of fear. Give me mine armour.
How does your patient, doctor?

*I'll go ahead and put it on.
Send out more horses. Search the entire
country and hang those who talk about fear.
Give me my armor. How is your patient,
doctor?*

Doctor
Not so sick, my lord,
As she is troubled with thick coming fancies,
That keep her from her rest.

*She's not so sick, my lord, as she is troubled
with numerous visions that keep her from
sleep.*

MACBETH
Cure her of that.
Canst thou not minister to a mind diseased,
Pluck from the memory a rooted sorrow,
Raze out the written troubles of the brain

*Cure her of that.
Can't you treat a diseased mind?
Can't you take away the memory rooted in
sorrows, carve out the troubles written in the*

And with some sweet oblivious antidote
Cleanse the stuff'd bosom of that perilous stuff
Which weighs upon the heart?

Doctor
Therein the patient
Must minister to himself.

MACBETH
Throw physic to the dogs; I'll none of it.
Come, put mine armour on; give me my staff.
Seyton, send out. Doctor, the thanes fly from me.
Come, sir, dispatch. If thou couldst, doctor, cast
The water of my land, find her disease,
And purge it to a sound and pristine health,
I would applaud thee to the very echo,
That should applaud again.--Pull't off, I say.--
What rhubarb, cyme, or what purgative drug,
Would scour these English hence?
Hear'st thou of them?

Doctor
Ay, my good lord; your royal preparation
Makes us hear something.

MACBETH
Bring it after me.
I will not be afraid of death and bane,
Till Birnam forest come to Dunsinane.

Doctor
[Aside] Were I from Dunsinane away and clear,
Profit again should hardly draw me here.

Exeunt

brain and with a sweet drug that causes oblivion and cleans out the dangerous stuff that weighs upon her heart?

*In that regard,
the patient must cure herself.*

Throw medicine to the dogs, then. I'll have none of it. Come, put my armor on me. Give me my staff. Seyton, send out. Doctor, the thanes leave me. Come sir, let's hurry. Can you figure out, doctor, what is wrong with my country? Check its urine, and return it to a sound and pristine health. I would applaud you to the very end, and the applause will echo back.—I'm telling you, pull it off— what plant or drug would send the English from this country? Have you heard of any?

Yes, my good lord. Your royal preparation for war makes us hear something.

*Bring it after me.
I will not be afraid of death and destruction until the Birnam forest comes to Dunsinane.*

[Aside] If I were far away from Dunsinane and clear of it, nothing could draw me back here again.

Scene IV

Country Near Birnam Wood

Drum and colours. Enter MALCOLM, SIWARD and YOUNG SIWARD, MACDUFF, MENTEITH, CAITHNESS, ANGUS, LENNOX, ROSS, and Soldiers, marching

MALCOLM
Cousins, I hope the days are near at hand
That chambers will be safe.

Cousins, I hope the days are near at hand when people will be safe in their homes.

MENTEITH
We doubt it nothing.

We don't doubt it.

SIWARD
What wood is this before us?

What is this wood before us?

MENTEITH
The wood of Birnam.

It's Birnam wood.

MALCOLM
Let every soldier hew him down a bough
And bear't before him: thereby shall we shadow
The numbers of our host and make discovery
Err in report of us.

Every soldier should cut off a tree limb and carry it before him. That way we will conceal how many of us there are and cause false reports about our numbers.

Soldiers
It shall be done.

We will do it.

SIWARD
We learn no other but the confident tyrant
Keeps still in Dunsinane, and will endure
Our setting down before 't.

We've heard nothing except the confident tyrant is still in Dunsinane, and will endure our attacking the castle.

MALCOLM
'Tis his main hope:
For where there is advantage to be given,
Both more and less have given him the revolt,
And none serve with him but constrained things
Whose hearts are absent too.

*That is his hope.
Whenever there is a chance, his soldiers revolt and leave him. None serve with him except for the severely restricted men whose hearts are not in it.*

MACDUFF
Let our just censures
Attend the true event, and put we on
Industrious soldiership.

*Let's not judge.
Keep your focus on the outcome, and continue being hard-working soldiers.*

SIWARD
The time approaches
That will with due decision make us know
What we shall say we have and what we owe.
Thoughts speculative their unsure hopes relate,
But certain issue strokes must arbitrate:
Towards which advance the war.

Exeunt, marching

The time is approaching
Soon we will discover what we have
and what we owe. We can speculate
on this and have uncertain hopes,
but the only certain way to find out
is to move forward toward battle

Scene V

Dunsinane. Within the Castle.

Enter MACBETH, SEYTON, and Soldiers, with drum and colours

MACBETH
Hang out our banners on the outward walls;
The cry is still 'They come:' our castle's strength
Will laugh a siege to scorn: here let them lie
Till famine and the ague eat them up:
Were they not forced with those that
should be ours, We might have met them dareful,
beard to beard, And beat them backward home.

A cry of women within

What is that noise?

SEYTON
It is the cry of women, my good lord.

Exit

MACBETH
I have almost forgot the taste of fears;
The time has been, my senses would have cool'd
To hear a night-shriek; and my fell of hair
Would at a dismal treatise rouse and stir
As life were in't: I have supp'd full with horrors;
Direness, familiar to my slaughterous thoughts
Cannot once start me.

Re-enter SEYTON

Wherefore was that cry?

SEYTON
The queen, my lord, is dead.

MACBETH
She should have died hereafter;
There would have been a time for such a word.
To-morrow, and to-morrow, and to-morrow,
Creeps in this petty pace from day to day
To the last syllable of recorded time,

Hang our flags on the outer walls of the castle. The cry is still 'They come.' Our castle's strength will laugh an attack to ridicule. Let them stay here until famine and illness eat them up. If our own soldiers hadn't run off to join them, we might have met them face to face, and beat them back toward their home.

What is that noise?

It is the women crying, my good lord.

I have almost forgotten the taste of fear. There would have been a time I'd have chills run through me at the sound of a shriek in the night, and the hair on my arms would have stood up during the telling of a frightening tale. As it is, I am so filled with horror it is familiar to me. Nothing can shock me.

What was that cry about?

The queen, my lord, is dead.

She would have died anyway. We would have heard it sooner or later. Tomorrow, or the next day, or the next. The days just keep moving forward until the end of time. The past has shown many fools the way to die.

And all our yesterdays have lighted fools
The way to dusty death. Out, out, brief candle!
Life's but a walking shadow, a poor player
That struts and frets his hour upon the stage
And then is heard no more: it is a tale
Told by an idiot, full of sound and fury,
Signifying nothing.

Enter a Messenger

Thou comest to use thy tongue; thy story quickly.

Messenger
Gracious my lord,
I should report that which I say I saw,
But know not how to do it.

MACBETH
Well, say, sir.

Messenger
As I did stand my watch upon the hill,
I look'd toward Birnam, and anon, methought,
The wood began to move.

MACBETH
Liar and slave!

Messenger
Let me endure your wrath, if't be not so:
Within this three mile may you see it coming;
I say, a moving grove.

MACBETH
If thou speak'st false,
Upon the next tree shalt thou hang alive,
Till famine cling thee: if thy speech be sooth,
I care not if thou dost for me as much.
I pull in resolution, and begin
To doubt the equivocation of the fiend
That lies like truth: 'Fear not, till Birnam wood
Do come to Dunsinane:' and now a wood
Comes toward Dunsinane. Arm, arm, and out!
If this which he avouches does appear,
There is nor flying hence nor tarrying here.
I gin to be aweary of the sun,

*Life is short! Life is brief! It's like a shadow,
like a bad actor walking around on the stage,
shouting and strutting as if he's oh so
important. Then, one day, he's just gone, and
you don't hear from him anymore. That's
when you realize it really meant nothing. All
of that shouting and anger —it meant nothing.*

*You're here to tell me something. Tell me,
already.*

*My gracious lord,
I should tell you that which I saw,
But I don't know how to do it.*

Just say it, sir.

*As I was standing my watch upon the hill
I looked toward Birnam, and—believe it or
not— I thought I saw the woods began to
move.*

Liar and slave!

*I will endure your anger if it's not true.
Within three miles you can see it coming—
a moving forest.*

*If you are lying, you will hang from
the nearest tree until hunger kills you.
If what you say is true, I don't care
if you do the same to me. My resolve
is failing. I'm beginning to doubt
the tricky language of the spirits
that lie that truth: 'Fear not, until
Birnam Wood comes to Dunsinane.'
And now a wood comes toward Dunsinane.
Get armed and let's go out!
If what the messenger says is true,
it's no use either way—running away*

And wish the estate o' the world were now undone.
Ring the alarum-bell! Blow, wind! come, wrack!
At least we'll die with harness on our back.

Exeunt

or staying here. I am growing weary of the sun, and I'd like to see the entire world destroyed. Ring the alarm! Blow, wind! Come, ruin! At least I'll die with armor on my back.

Scene VI.

Dunsinane. Before the Castle.

Drum and colours. Enter MALCOLM, SIWARD, MACDUFF, and their Army, with boughs

MALCOLM
Now near enough: your leafy screens throw down.
And show like those you are. You, worthy uncle,
Shall, with my cousin, your right-noble son,
Lead our first battle: worthy Macduff and we
Shall take upon 's what else remains to do,
According to our order.

Now that we are near enough, throw down you boughs and show yourself as you are. Worthy uncle, you will—with my cousin, your son—lead our first battle. Worthy Macduff and I will do what remains to be done, according to our battle orders.

SIWARD
Fare you well.
Do we but find the tyrant's power to-night,
Let us be beaten, if we cannot fight.

Good luck.
If we find the tyrant's armies tonight, let us be beaten if we cannot fight.

MACDUFF
Make all our trumpets speak; give them all breath,
Those clamorous harbingers of blood and death.

Blow all of our trumpets. Make them loud. They are the noisy announcers of blood and death.

Exeunt

Scene VII

Another Part of the Field.

Alarums. Enter MACBETH

MACBETH
They have tied me to a stake; I cannot fly,
But, bear-like, I must fight the course. What's he
That was not born of woman? Such a one
Am I to fear, or none.

They have tied me to a stake. I cannot run.
Bear-like, I must fight.
Who is he that was not born of a woman?
That is the only one I am to fear.

Enter YOUNG SIWARD

YOUNG SIWARD
What is thy name?

What is your name?

MACBETH
Thou'lt be afraid to hear it.

You'll be afraid once you hear it.

YOUNG SIWARD
No; though thou call'st thyself a hotter name
Than any is in hell.

No, I won't, even if it's the worst name
than any that is in hell.

MACBETH
My name's Macbeth.

My name is Macbeth.

YOUNG SIWARD
The devil himself could not pronounce a title
More hateful to mine ear.

The devil himself does not have a name
that I hate more to hear.

MACBETH
No, nor more fearful.

No, and the devil's name wouldn't be more
frightening.

YOUNG SIWARD
Thou liest, abhorred tyrant; with my sword
I'll prove the lie thou speak'st.

You lie, hated tyrant. I will prove to you
with my sword that I am not afraid of you.

They fight and YOUNG SIWARD is slain

MACBETH
Thou wast born of woman
But swords I smile at, weapons laugh to scorn,
Brandish'd by man that's of a woman born.

You were born of a woman.
I laugh at weapons waved
by a man who was born of a woman.

Exit

Alarums. Enter MACDUFF

MACDUFF
That way the noise is. Tyrant, show thy face!
If thou be'st slain and with no stroke of mine,
My wife and children's ghosts will haunt me still.
I cannot strike at wretched kerns, whose arms
Are hired to bear their staves: either thou, Macbeth,
Or else my sword with an unbatter'd edge
I sheathe again undeeded. There thou shouldst be;
By this great clatter, one of greatest note
Seems bruited. Let me find him, fortune!
And more I beg not.

The noise comes from over there. Tyrant, show your face! If you are killed and I do not make the stroke that kills you. my wife and children's ghosts will haunt me forever. I cannot waste my time fighting foot soldiers who are paid to carry their swords. It's either you, Macbeth, or I will put my sword away un-used. That's where you should be, by the great noise coming from there it sounds like someone of note is being announced. Let me find him! I will not ask for more.

Exit. Alarums

Enter MALCOLM and SIWARD

SIWARD
This way, my lord; the castle's gently render'd:
The tyrant's people on both sides do fight;
The noble thanes do bravely in the war;
The day almost itself professes yours,
And little is to do.

Come this way, my lord. The castle has been surrendered. The tyrant's people fight for both sides. The noble thanes are fighting bravely. Victory is near, and there is little more to do.

MALCOLM
We have met with foes
That strike beside us.

We have met with foes who fight as if they are with us.

SIWARD
Enter, sir, the castle.

Enter the castle, sir.

Exeunt. Alarums

Scene VIII

Another Part of the Field.

Enter MACBETH

MACBETH
Why should I play the Roman fool, and die
On mine own sword? whiles I see lives, the gashes
Do better upon them.

Why should I play the Roman fool, and die by my own sword? As long as I sees others living, the wounds will be better on them.

Enter MACDUFF

MACDUFF
Turn, hell-hound, turn!

Turn around, you hell-hound, turn around!

MACBETH
Of all men else I have avoided thee:
But get thee back; my soul is too much charged
With blood of thine already.

Of all the men I've avoided seeing, it is you. But go away, now—my soul is already charged with the blood of your entire family.

MACDUFF
I have no words:
My voice is in my sword: thou bloodier villain
Than terms can give thee out!

I have nothing to say. My voice is in my sword. You are more evil than any words could say.

They fight

MACBETH
Thou losest labour:
As easy mayst thou the intrenchant air
With thy keen sword impress as make me bleed:
Let fall thy blade on vulnerable crests;
I bear a charmed life, which must not yield,
To one of woman born.

You waste your labor. You might as well try to slash the air with your sword. You will not make me bleed. I live a charmed life, and it will not yield to a man born of woman.

MACDUFF
Despair thy charm;
And let the angel whom thou still hast served
Tell thee, Macduff was from his mother's womb
Untimely ripp'd.

Lose hope about that charm, Macbeth. Let the evil spirit who served you with that information tell you: Macduff was ripped from his mother's womb prematurely.

MACBETH
Accursed be that tongue that tells me so,
For it hath cow'd my better part of man!
And be these juggling fiends no more believed,

Curse you for telling me this! It has made me into a coward! These deceptive evil spirits are not to be believed. They talk insincerely

That palter with us in a double sense;
That keep the word of promise to our ear,
And break it to our hope. I'll not fight with thee.

*in a way that makes no sense. They made
promises to me, then dashed my hopes.
I won't fight with you.*

MACDUFF
Then yield thee, coward,
And live to be the show and gaze o' the time:
We'll have thee, as our rarer monsters are,
Painted on a pole, and underwrit,
'Here may you see the tyrant.'

*Then give up, you coward,
and live to be a freak in a show to be looked at
all the time like other monsters. We'll post a
likeness of you on a pole with the words
underneath: 'You can see the tyrant here.'*

MACBETH
I will not yield,
To kiss the ground before young Malcolm's feet,
And to be baited with the rabble's curse.
Though Birnam wood be come to Dunsinane,
And thou opposed, being of no woman born,
Yet I will try the last. Before my body
I throw my warlike shield. Lay on, Macduff,
And damn'd be him that first cries, 'Hold, enough!'

*I will not yield to you, only to kiss
the ground at young Malcolm's feet,
or tormented by the common people.
Yes, Birnam wood did come to Dunsinane,
and I am fighting a man not born of woman.
Still, I will fight to the end. I put up my shield
to battle you. Come on, Macduff, and damned
be the one who cries first 'Stop, enough!'*

*Exeunt, fighting. Alarums
Retreat. Flourish. Enter, with drum and colours, MALCOLM, SIWARD, ROSS, the other Thanes,
and Soldiers*

MALCOLM
I would the friends we miss were safe arrived.

*I wish the friends we miss could have
survived.*

SIWARD
Some must go off: and yet, by these I see,
So great a day as this is cheaply bought.

*Some are lost in every battle, but by the ones
I see, this victory didn't cost much in lives.*

MALCOLM
Macduff is missing, and your noble son.

Macduff is missing, and your noble son.

ROSS
Your son, my lord, has paid a soldier's debt:
He only lived but till he was a man;
The which no sooner had his prowess confirm'd
In the unshrinking station where he fought,
But like a man he died.

*Your son, my lord, has paid a soldier's debt.
He only lived until he was a man, and no
sooner was his skill as a fighter obvious in the
fearless way he fought—
he died like a man.*

SIWARD
Then he is dead?

So he is dead?

ROSS
Ay, and brought off the field: your cause of sorrow
Must not be measured by his worth, for then
It hath no end.

Yes, and he has been brought off the field.
Your grief should not be measured by his
worth, or it will never end.

SIWARD
Had he his hurts before?

Was he wounded on the front?

ROSS
Ay, on the front.

Yes, on the front.

SIWARD
Why then, God's soldier be he!
Had I as many sons as I have hairs,
I would not wish them to a fairer death:
And so, his knell is knoll'd.

Well then, he is God's soldier!
If I had as many sons as I have hairs,
I would not wish them a better death.
So, his funeral bell shall be rung.

MALCOLM
He's worth more sorrow,
And that I'll spend for him.

He is worth more grief than that.
I will spend it for him.

SIWARD
He's worth no more
They say he parted well, and paid his score:
And so, God be with him!
Here comes newer comfort.

He's worth no more.
They say he went quickly, and settled his
score. So, God be with him!
Here comes new comfort.

Re-enter MACDUFF, with MACBETH's head

MACDUFF
Hail, king! for so thou art: behold, where stands
The usurper's cursed head: the time is free:
I see thee compass'd with thy kingdom's pearl,
That speak my salutation in their minds;
Whose voices I desire aloud with mine:
Hail, King of Scotland!

Hail, king! That's what you are now. Look,
here is the offender's cursed head. We are
free now. I see you are surrounded by the
kingdom's best, and they speak in my mind
what I want to say. I want them to join me in
saying: Hail, King of Scotland!

ALL
Hail, King of Scotland!

Hail, King of Scotland!

Flourish

MALCOLM
We shall not spend a large expense of time
Before we reckon with your several loves,
And make us even with you.

We will not spend a large amount of time,
before we figure out your honors, and make
us even with you.

My thanes and kinsmen,
Henceforth be earls, the first that ever Scotland
In such an honour named. What's more to do,
Which would be planted newly with the time,
As calling home our exiled friends abroad
That fled the snares of watchful tyranny;
Producing forth the cruel ministers
Of this dead butcher and his fiend-like queen,
Who, as 'tis thought, by self and violent hands
Took off her life; this, and what needful else
That calls upon us, by the grace of Grace,
We will perform in measure, time and place:
So, thanks to all at once and to each one,
Whom we invite to see us crown'd at Scone.

Flourish. Exeunt

My thanes and kinsmen—
you will be earls, the first that Scotland
has ever known. There's more to do in this
new time. We must call home our exiled
friends who are abroad, having fled the
devices of a watchful tyranny, and we must
bring forth the cruel agents of this dead
butcher and his evil wife, who it is said took
her own life. This, and whatever else is
needed, we will perform by the grace of God
in measure, time and place. Thanks to
everyone and to each one,
who we invite to see us
crowned at Scone.

Lightning Source UK Ltd.
Milton Keynes UK
UKHW031110050419
340546UK00004B/493/P